FINDING JESUS
IN EVERYDAY MOMENTS

100-Day Devotional Journal for Women

FINDING JESUS IN *Everyday* MOMENTS

ANNE CETAS

from Our Daily Bread

Our Daily Bread
Publishing™

Cover Design: Emily Weigel

Library of Congress Cataloging-in-Publication Data

Names: Cetas, Anne, author.
Title: Finding Jesus in everyday moments : 100-day devotional journal for women / Anne Cetas from Our Daily Bread.
Description: Grand Rapids : Our Daily Bread Publishing, [2021] | Summary: "Reflect on God's presence in your life through 100 story-driven, Bible-focused devotionals"-- Provided by publisher.
Identifiers: LCCN 2020038915 | ISBN 9781640700857
Subjects: LCSH: Meditations.
Classification: LCC BV4832.3 .C426 2021 | DDC 242/.643--dc23
LC record available at https://lccn.loc.gov/2020038915

ISBN: 978-1-64070-085-7

Printed in the United States of America

21 22 23 24 25 26 27 28 29 / 9 8 7 6 5 4 3

FOREWORD

If you are a regular reader of *Our Daily Bread*, you are no doubt familiar with the writings of Anne Cetas. She's been sharing her insights with readers for more than fifteen years. Anne has a rich history with the ministry as well as a life of service outside the doors of the office. And she's been my dear friend for more than thirty-five years.

As a young woman in the 1980s, she took a position as my dad's secretary in the editorial department. Admittedly, the qualification that impressed him most was that she could type one hundred words a minute. (Yes, *type*, a vital role in the business office before the age of personal computers.) Clair Hess had no idea Anne's gifts ran even deeper than that. However, he soon discovered that his secretary had an innate talent for proofreading. That soon grew into a mastery of the art form we call "editing." During those early days, Anne had the privilege of working with and being mentored by some of the well-loved editors of *Our Daily Bread*, including people like Dennis DeHaan, Dave Branon, and Kurt DeHaan.

Anne has a heart for people of all ages. In her writings, she humbly shares what she's learned from encounters with people in all walks of life, but often they are people from communities that are ignored or underserved by society at large. She readily admits that she gains a lot of joy in the people she has come to know, ranging from nursery-age kiddos to senior citizens.

Every Saturday night for about twenty years, she and her husband, Carl, have gathered with children for a ministry at their church. They played games, mentored the kids, and taught them about God's love. As the children grew up, the bond that had been forged continued, and Anne and Carl are often invited to graduations and weddings and baby showers. In recent years, Anne has become involved with a refugee ministry, becoming a compassionate friend to people who are displaced, don't speak English, and are struggling to adjust to a new country. The Google Translator app comes in handy!

I have to admit that I don't really understand Anne's fierce love of baseball, football, basketball, and other sports. Even though I did watch every minute of *Field of Dreams* once, I'm still pretty ignorant of most things sport-related. Not Anne and Carl though. Any free Saturday during baseball season, they'd be thrilled to drive to the east side of the state of Michigan to watch the Detroit Tigers play. They are such devoted fans that when the old Tiger Stadium was demolished in 2008, they salvaged two metal stadium seats that now sit in their TV room as a memento of the good times they had at the corner of Michigan and Trumbull in Motown.

Anne and I do share a love for oldies music (mostly the 1970s). We've sat in the nose-bleed section for a few concerts and learned early on not to take binoculars along to see the stage. (Aging rockers are not pretty.) And we've been known to have a whole email conversation made up entirely of song lyrics.

The point is, Anne is real. She is genuine. She doesn't hide her doubts or pain or disappointment. Readers of *Our Daily Bread* find her voice empathizing with their own struggles because she's not reluctant to tussle with God over the difficult questions: *Why didn't God restore her sister Carolyn to health? Why did He allow a car crash that took her friend Sharon home to heaven?* Her authentic pondering of life's difficulties mirrors our own as we deal with questions of injustice, sorrow, guilt, or confusion.

My friend Anne loves Jesus, and her articles are liberally sprinkled with Bible stories about Him and the gospel of salvation He has provided us. You will find that her observations about the Lord can bring you times of reflection about how having a personal relationship with Him changes everything. "Jesus Moments" abound in Anne's articles, and I think they will help you love Him and serve Him even more than you already do. Her writing gently leads us to our Savior Jesus, His goodness, His care for us, His promise never to leave us, and the unexpected blessings He has in mind for us.

—Cindy Hess Kasper
Former editor, Our Daily Bread Ministries

1

Unexpected Encounter

The Context: Psalm 42

Since, then, you have been raised with Christ,
set your hearts on things above. —Paul, *Colossians 3:1*

When my close friend Sharon was killed in a car accident, my heart broke. I don't like admitting it, but when life's circumstances hurt so much, my faith is often mixed with doubt. When Sharon died, I cried out to God with these questions:

Lord, I sure don't understand you. Why did you allow this death? "Have you not heard? The LORD . . . will not grow tired or weary, and his understanding no one can fathom" (Isaiah 40:28). "My thoughts are not your thoughts, neither are your ways my ways" (55:8).

Lord, you are beyond my understanding. But I still wonder, have you turned your back on the world? "God is seated on his holy throne" (Psalm 47:8) and "rules forever by his power" (66:7).

Lord, I do believe you are ruling this world, but do you care about the pain? Have you forgotten my pain? Jesus offers: "Come to me, all you who are weary and burdened, and I will give you rest" (Matthew 11:28).

Yes, Lord, you have been good to me in countless ways, including listening to my doubts and questions about you. Even when we have an unexpected encounter of the worst kind, we can trust in you.

> Every loss leaves an empty space that
> only God's presence can fill.

Jesus Moment

Recall an unexpected encounter in your life. What are two or three prayer questions you would like to talk to your Savior about?

_____

_____

_____

_____

_____

Key Words from the Word

"Fear not, for I am with you; be not dismayed, for I am your God; I will strengthen you, I will help you, I will uphold you with my righteous right hand." —*God, Isaiah 41:10 ESV*

"The LORD is my shepherd; I shall not want. He makes me to lie down in green pastures; He leads me beside the still waters. He restores my soul." —*David, Psalm 23:1–3 NKJV*

"When the righteous cry for help, the LORD hears and delivers them out of all their troubles. The LORD is near to the broken-hearted and saves the crushed in spirit."
—*David, Psalm 34:17–18 ESV*

"Praise be to the God and Father of our Lord Jesus Christ, the Father of compassion and the God of all comfort, who comforts us in all our troubles, so that we can comfort those in any trouble."
—*Paul, 2 Corinthians 1:3–4*

2

Surprise Blessing

The Context: Acts 9:1–19

I became a servant of this gospel by the gift of God's grace
given me through the working of his power. —Paul, Ephesians 3:7

A woman from Grand Rapids, Michigan, fell asleep on the couch after her husband had gone to bed. An intruder sneaked in through the sliding door, which the couple had forgotten to lock, and crept through the house. He entered the bedroom where the husband was sleeping and picked up the television set. The sleeping man woke up, saw a figure standing there, and whispered, "Honey, come to bed." The burglar panicked, put down the TV, grabbed a stack of money from the dresser, and ran out.

The thief was in for a big surprise! The money turned out to be a stack of Christian pamphlets with a likeness of a $20 bill on one side and an explanation of the love and forgiveness God offers to people on the other side. Instead of the cash he expected, the intruder got the story of God's love for him.

I wonder what Saul expected when he realized it was Jesus appearing to him on the road to Damascus, since he had been persecuting and even killing Jesus's followers (Acts 9:1–9)? Saul, who we now know as the apostle Paul, must have been surprised by God's grace toward him, which he later called "a gift": "I became a servant of this gospel by the gift of God's grace given me through the working of his power" (Ephesians 3:7).

Have you been surprised by the blessing of the Lord's gift of grace in your life as He shows you His love and forgiveness?

Jesus Moment

Think of how the Lord is pouring out His blessings in ways you were not expecting. How can you thank Him for that?

_____

_____

_____

_____

_____

Lyrics for the Heart

'Twas grace that taught my heart to fear,
And grace my fears relieved;
How precious did that grace appear
The hour I first believed!

—"Amazing Grace," John Newton (1725-1807)

Never measure God's unlimited power
by your limited expectations.

3

Jesus's Very Own Peace

The Context: Matthew 16:21–23

Peace I leave with you; my peace I give you.
I do not give to you as the world gives. —Jesus, John 14:27

On the eve of the execution of Christian martyr Nicholas Ridley (1500–1555), his brother offered to stay with him in prison to be of comfort. Ridley declined, saying that he planned to sleep as soundly as usual. Because he knew the peace of Jesus, he could rest in his Lord.

The next morning, Ridley told a fellow Christian who was also being executed, "Be of good heart, brother, for God will either assuage the fury of the flame, or else strengthen us to abide it." Then they knelt and prayed by the stake. After a brief conversation, they were burned to death for their faith.

Jesus had given Nicholas Ridley His peace (John 14:27). But what kind of peace did Jesus have? In Matthew 16:21–23, we see His peace in His determination to go to Jerusalem even though He knew He would suffer and die (see Luke 9:51). Peter rebuked Him, but Jesus trusted His Father and went to the cross. His purpose for living was to die for us.

Amy Carmichael said, "The peace of Jesus stood every sort of test, every strain, and it never broke. It is this, His very own peace, which He says, 'I give.'"

No matter how big or small our trials may be, we can trust Jesus to give us His very own peace in the midst of them.

Jesus Moment

Although Jesus said, "Let not your heart be troubled," perhaps something is bothering you right now. How can you put that burden on Jesus's shoulders and have His peace?

_____

_____

_____

_____

_____

Inspiring Words

"When we live in peace with God, we are eager to make peace with others." —*Julie Ackerman Link, American author (1950–2015)*

"Those persons who know the deep peace of God, the unfathomable peace that passes all understanding, are always men and women of much prayer."
—*R. A. Torrey, American evangelist (1856–1928)*

"If peace seems elusive in your life today, commit yourself to God, commit your concerns to Him in prayer, and then rest peacefully as you trust in Him." —*David Jeremiah, American pastor (1941–)*

When Jesus rules the heart, peace reigns.

4

Come to Me

The Context: John 6:30–40

I am the bread of life. Whoever comes to me will never go hungry, and whoever believes in me will never be thirsty. —Jesus, John 6:35

When Jesus lived on this earth, He invited people to come to Him, and He still does today (John 6:35). What do He and His Father in heaven have that we need?

Salvation. Jesus is the only way to have forgiveness of sin and the promise of heaven. "Whoever believes in Him should not perish but have eternal life" (John 3:15 NKJV).

Purpose. We are to give all of our heart, soul, mind, and strength to following Jesus. "Whoever wants to be my disciple must deny themselves and take up their cross and follow me" (Mark 8:34).

Comfort. In trial or sorrow, the "God of all comfort . . . comforts us in all our troubles" (2 Corinthians 1:3–4).

Wisdom. We need wisdom for making decisions. "If any of you lacks wisdom, you should ask God, . . . and it will be given to you" (James 1:5).

Strength. When we're weary, "the LORD gives strength to his people" (Psalm 29:11).

Abundant Life. The fullest life is found in a relationship with Jesus. "I have come that they may have life, and have it to the full" (John 10:10).

Jesus said, "Whoever comes to me I will never drive away" (John 6:37). Come!

Jesus invites us to come to Him for life.

Jesus Moment

When was the last time you and Jesus "sat down" for some time together? What do you want to say just to Him? What do you think He is telling you about himself or what you need from Him?

_____

_____

_____

_____

_____

Thinking about What God Gives

- God has provided salvation through Jesus. What are some ways that reality in your life has made you who you are today?

_____

_____

- God provides wisdom through His Word and through the Holy Spirit. In what areas of life right now do you most need His wisdom to guide you?

_____

_____

- God promises strength for His people. When you feel weak, what can you do to regain the strength of God in your life?

_____

_____

5

Cherished Connections

The Context: 1 John 4:7–5:1

In Christ we, though many, form one body,
and each member belongs to all the others. —Paul, Romans 12:5

When I heard that David was in the office of our ministry for a board meeting, I was excited. He and I had a mutual friend, Sharon, who had died several years earlier. We had a few minutes to reminisce about her and her love for life and God. What a delight to connect with someone who has loved someone you have loved! There's a special bond because you love to talk about that cherished person.

Those of us who know Jesus Christ as Savior have even stronger ties. We are forever connected to Him and to one another. "In Christ we, though many, form one body, and each member belongs to all the others," Paul says in Romans 12:5. We've been "born of God," and we love those who are "begotten of Him" (1 John 5:1 NKJV).

When we get together with fellow believers, we have the opportunity to talk about the one we love—Christ—and of the love, forgiveness, and grace we have experienced in Him because of His death and resurrection (4:9–10). At such times, we can encourage each other to continue to trust Him and spur one another on to be faithful in our walk with Him.

This coming Sunday and throughout the week, let's remind fellow believers of all that Jesus has done and of how truly wonderful He is.

Jesus Moment

Who are a couple of friends you can talk to about your love for and relationship with Jesus? Should you get together soon to be amazed all over again by Jesus?

_____

_____

_____

_____

_____

_____

Communicating with Jesus

Dear Lord in heaven, help us to direct both our thoughts and our conversations toward you. Help us to take every opportunity to speak of you at the appropriate times. Guide our tongues to mention you in discussing life with our Christian friends. And give us boldness to find ways to talk of you with our friends and relatives—and when appropriate, our coworkers who don't know you. Thank you for the guidance of the Spirit as we speak of you with others. Amen.

> The more you love Jesus,
> the more you'll talk about Him.

6

Lost Treasure

The Context: Mark 10:17–27

Jesus looked at him and loved him. "One thing you lack," he said. "Go, sell everything you have and give to the poor, and you will have treasure in heaven. Then come, follow me." —Jesus, Mark 10:21

Don takes walks on the city's railroad tracks and searches under freeway overpasses. He's not looking for lost treasure; he's looking for homeless people. One day Don met Jake, who lives in a makeshift underground shack and is mentally ill. Now Don stops by to see Jake occasionally, making sure he's warm and has food. He tells Jake about Jesus because he wants him to find "treasure in heaven" (Mark 10:21).

Jesus talked about this treasure with a rich young man who asked Him how to inherit eternal life. Jesus said, "Sell everything you have and give to the poor, and you will have treasure in heaven. Then come, follow me" (10:21).

Jesus wasn't teaching that we must give up our wealth to be acceptable to Him. We can never earn eternal life by our works. He was showing this man his spiritual bankruptcy. His heart was set on wealth, not Jesus.

That rich young man and our homeless friend have more in common than we might think. In the eyes of God, both are spiritually bankrupt. We all are, unless we have Jesus.

No good deed can earn eternal life—not helping the homeless or giving away all our money. Jesus wants us to give Him our heart. Then we'll have real treasure—treasure in heaven—and we'll seek to help others.

Jesus Moment

Does Jesus have your heart? How can you make Him your first priority—even as you attend to so many other good things in your life?

_____

_____

_____

_____

_____

Communicating with God

Dear heavenly Father, I understand that my first priority is to allow my heart to be filled with Jesus and His love. Help me to surrender myself to Him. Then, as I allow Him to rule, guide me to those areas of service where I can be of some good to the kingdom of God. Show me how I can use my life of commitment to Jesus to be of assistance to others physically, emotionally, and spiritually.

Salvation is given, not earned.

Working in the Harvest

The Context: Matthew 9:35–10:7

Ask the Lord of the harvest, therefore,
to send out workers into his harvest field. —*Jesus, Matthew 9:38*

While Dwight L. Moody (1837–1899) was attending a convention in Indianapolis on mass evangelism, he did more than just talk about it. He asked a friend, who was a gifted musician, to meet him on a street corner at six o'clock one evening. The man stood on a box and sang a song. When a crowd gathered, Moody spoke briefly and then invited the people to follow him to the nearby convention hall.

Soon the auditorium was filled with spiritually hungry people, and Moody preached to them. When the convention attendees began to arrive, he stopped preaching and said, "Now we must close, as the brethren of the convention want to discuss the topic, 'How to reach the masses.'"

When Jesus saw the crowds, He "had compassion on them" (Matthew 9:36). He said to His disciples, "The harvest is plentiful. . . . Ask the Lord of the harvest, therefore, to send out workers" (vv. 37–38). And He sent them out to preach the good news of His kingdom (10:5–7).

It is estimated that only ten percent of the world's population of nearly eight billion are believers in Jesus Christ. And more than twenty-five percent have never heard of Jesus's love even once.

As Jesus's disciples today, let's not just talk about the need—let's pray and go.

The next person you meet might be your mission field.

Jesus Moment

Ask Jesus to point out to you at least one person who needs to know about His love and forgiveness. Then ask Him to help you know how to introduce her to Jesus. What are some possible ways to do that?

_____

_____

_____

_____

_____

_____

Action Steps

As you think about being a worker in God's harvest fields, which specific action steps could you begin to explore?

_____ Looking around your neighborhood for someone you can introduce to Jesus.

_____ Finding a way to use social media to let others know about your Savior.

_____ Praying for God to lead you toward someone who needs a kind gesture or word in Jesus's name.

_____ Making a concerted effort to spread the joy of Jesus in day-to-day interactions with others at the store, at school, at work, at appointments.

_____ *Another idea:* _____

_____

8

A Pleasant Diversion

The Context: Romans 11:33–12:2

Do not conform to the pattern of this world, but be transformed
by the renewing of your mind. Then you will be able to test and approve
what God's will is—his good, pleasing and perfect will. —*Paul, Romans 12:2*

A friend who was looking for a church to join told me she had found just what she wanted: "I like this church because I don't have to change my lifestyle of partying. It doesn't make me feel guilty or require anything of me. It makes me feel good about myself."

Author W. Waldo Beach calls this kind of church "a pleasant weekend diversion."

But is this what Jesus calls us to? Beach says, "No amount of air-conditioning and pew-cushioning . . . can cover over the hard truth that . . . discipleship is costly; that, for the faithful, there is always a cross to be carried. No one can understand Christianity to its depths who comes to it to enjoy it as a pleasant weekend diversion."

Being a Christian means that we know Jesus personally. We have received Him by faith as our Savior from sin, and we present ourselves to Him. We deny our will and choose His instead. He transforms our thinking, our values, and our priorities to reflect what is acceptable to God (Romans 12:1–2).

Is your religion just a pleasant weekend diversion? That's no substitute for a vital relationship with Jesus!

Jesus Moment

Think of ways your mind sometimes conforms to the pattern of the world around you. How does religion sometimes replace Jesus in your life? What spiritual activities can help change that?

_____

_____

_____

_____

_____

Key Words from the Word

"Whoever wants to be my disciple must deny themselves and take up their cross daily and follow me." —*Jesus, Luke 9:23*

"Let the message of Christ dwell among you richly as you teach and admonish one another with all wisdom through psalms, hymns, and songs from the Spirit." —*Paul, Colossians 3:16*

"Those who belong to Christ Jesus have crucified the flesh with its passions and desires." —*Paul, Galatians 5:24*

Discipleship demands discipline.

9

Off-Limits

The Context: Romans 5:1–8

For God so loved the world that he gave his one and only Son, that whoever believes in him shall not perish but have eternal life. —John, John 3:16

As a twelve-year-old, I was curious about the Bible my dad was given when he retired from the paper mill. It came in a special cedar box marked The Holy Bible, and I assumed that "holy" meant it was off-limits to me. But still I peered inside. In the center of the Bible was a picture of Jesus hanging on the cross, along with the words of John 3:16. There was also a see-through red film covering the page, which I assumed meant He bled and died.

Occasionally, when no one else was looking, I would gently pull the holy Book off the shelf, open the box, look at the picture of Jesus on the cross, read the verse, and wonder about this Man and why He died. I wondered if His love was meant for me or if it too was off-limits.

Several years later I heard a message about how God had provided access to His love through Jesus. Romans 5:1–2 tells us: "We have peace with God through our Lord Jesus Christ, through whom we have gained access by faith into this grace in which we now stand." I believed and received Jesus's salvation from my sin.

Aren't you thankful that the Bible and God's love aren't off-limits? Receive His forgiveness—it's meant for unholy people like you and me.

Jesus Moment

What makes even good people unholy? And how is it that Jesus's death gives us His holiness? Have you gained "access by faith into [God's] grace"? You can trade your unholiness for God's holiness by trusting Jesus as Savior.

_____

_____

_____

_____

_____

Lyrics for the Heart

The love of God is greater far
Than tongue or pen can ever tell;
It goes beyond the highest star,
And reaches to the lowest hell;
O love of God, how rich and pure!
How measureless and strong!
It shall forevermore endure
The saints' and angels' song.

"The Love of God," Frederick Lehman (1868–1953)

The Bible is God's love letter to us.

Isn't He Beautiful!

The Context: Isaiah 9:1–7

> For to us a child is born, to us a son is given, and the government will be on his shoulders. And he will be called Wonderful Counselor, Mighty God, Everlasting Father, Prince of Peace. —*Isaiah, Isaiah 9:6*

A group of children from our city were in a worship service, and we started to sing. Ariel, age seven, leaned close to me and softly said, "I love this song; it makes me cry."

The music and words about Jesus, her Savior, touched her heart: The song asked about Jesus, reflecting on His beauty and reminding us that He is the Prince of Peace.

Yes, the Lord Jesus is beautiful. We don't find a specific reference in the Bible describing Him that way, but His personal character is strong yet gentle, holy yet forgiving, majestic yet humble—all combined. Simply beautiful!

In his prophecy, Isaiah described Jesus and His coming in this way: "For to us a child is born, to us a son is given, and the government will be on his shoulders. And he will be called Wonderful Counselor, Mighty God, Everlasting Father, Prince of Peace" (Isaiah 9:6).

Jesus is the Wonderful Counselor—giving us comfort and wisdom. The Mighty God—acting with power and authority. The Everlasting Father—providing for all our needs and protecting us. And the Prince of Peace—offering reconciliation with God and others.

Jesus Moment

Which of those magnificent titles in Isaiah 9:6 best captures the characteristic of Jesus that is most helpful to you right now?

_____

_____

_____

_____

_____

Communicating with Jesus

Dear Lord Jesus, because you are my Wonderful Counselor, I ask you to guide me today in my decisions and actions. Let what I say and do today be done according to your will. Because you are Mighty God, I praise you for this marvelous world and the role you have allowed me to play in it. Because you are the Everlasting Father, I ask for you to meet my daily needs. Because you are the Prince of Peace, I ask you to bring hope to those who don't know you and need your gracious peace.

Jesus is the image of the invisible God.

"Let's Go!"

The Context: Philippians 1:19–26

The twelve gates were twelve pearls, each gate made of a single pearl.
The great street of the city was of gold, as pure as transparent glass.
—John, Revelation 21:21

My nine-year-old neighbor Jasmine was sitting on the front porch with me one summer evening. Out of the blue she started talking about her bad choices and how she needed God's forgiveness. We talked and prayed together, and she asked Jesus to be her Savior.

Questions about heaven started pouring out of her: "Are the streets really gold? Will my mom be there? What if she isn't? Will I have a bed, or will I sleep on a cloud? What will I eat?" I assured her that heaven would be a perfect home and that she would be with Jesus, who would give her everything she needed. She replied with excitement, "Well, then, let's go right now!"

The apostle Paul had a heavenly perspective too (Philippians 1:23). He said, "For to me, to live is Christ and to die is gain" (v. 21). He knew that this life was about knowing, trusting, and serving God. But he also knew that life in heaven would be "better by far" because he would "be with Christ" (v. 23). He was ready to stay as a witness to others, but he was also ready to go see Jesus.

Jasmine is ready to go now. Are we as eager for heaven as she is?

Those who have their hearts fixed on heaven
will hold loosely to the things of earth.

Jesus Moment

Meditate for a moment about what it will be like to see Jesus and to be in His presence for the first time. What emotions touch your heart when you think about that amazing moment?

_____

_____

_____

_____

Thinking about Heaven

- What are two or three physical characteristics about heaven that you are curious about?

_____

_____

- And there are the people. Other than Jesus, who are three people you just can't wait to meet or see again?

_____

_____

- Is it good or bad that although we can't wait to see heaven, we also have some reservations about going there soon? Why?

_____

_____

12

Walking in His Dust

The Context: Mark 14:3–9

Without delay [Jesus] called them, and they left their father Zebedee in the boat with the hired men and followed him. —Mark, Mark 1:20

In the first century, a Jewish man who wanted to become a disciple of a rabbi (teacher) was expected to leave family and job to join his rabbi. They would live together twenty-four hours a day—walking from place to place, teaching and learning, studying and working. They discussed and memorized the Scriptures and applied them to life.

A disciple's calling, as described in early Jewish writings about basic ethics, was to "cover himself in the dust of [the rabbi's] feet," drinking in his every word. He followed his rabbi so closely that he would "walk in his dust." In doing so, he became like the rabbi, his master.

Simon, Andrew, James, and John knew that this was the type of relationship to which Jesus was calling them (Mark 1:16–20). So immediately they walked away from their work and "followed him" (v. 20). For three years they stayed close to Jesus—listening to His teaching, watching His miracles, learning His principles, and walking in His dust.

As Jesus's followers today, we too can "walk in His dust." By making it a priority to spend time studying and meditating on His Word and then applying its principles to our lives, we'll become like our rabbi—Jesus.

Jesus Moment

What does it mean to make it a priority to study God's Word? What steps can you take to do that, despite your busy schedule?

_____

_____

_____

_____

_____

Inspiring Words

"If Jesus is the Son of God, His teachings are more than just good ideas from a wise teacher; they are divine insights on which I can confidently build my life." —*Lee Strobel, American journalist*

"How could it be anything less than a joy to serve the One who has given us all things for life, and enrichment, and enjoyment?" —*Joni Eareckson Tada, American author, speaker*

"Experience is not the best teacher, Jesus is!" —*Unknown*

"Jesus is not some puny religious teacher begging for an invitation from anyone. He is the all-sovereign Lord who deserves submission from everyone." —*David Platt, American pastor*

> Faith in Christ is not just a single step—
> it is a lifelong walk with Him.

13

People of God

The Context: 1 Peter 2:1–10

Once you were not a people, but now you are the people of God;
once you had not received mercy, but now you have received mercy.
—Peter, 1 Peter 2:10

A little girl was being punished for bad behavior, and her parents were making her eat dinner by herself in the corner of the room. They paid no attention to her until they heard her pray part of Psalm 23: "I thank you, Lord, for preparing a table before me in the presence of my enemies."

A cute story, but our families can sometimes feel like our enemies when they aren't exactly what we want them to be. Even our spiritual family at church lets us down occasionally. But by changing our focus we can learn to give up the naïve idea that others will always meet our lofty expectations.

Instead of focusing on what others think, we can find hope in the truth that each of us is one of God's very own children through faith in Jesus (1 Peter 2:10). He has chosen us and made us "His own special people" (v. 9 NKJV). God has brought us into His family, and we can be sure that our relationship with Him will never be severed. He'll never treat us as an enemy.

When others let us down, instead of giving in to discouragement let's change our focus and remind ourselves that we who have put our faith in Jesus are God's children—cherished and cared for by Him.

Jesus Moment

How does it feel to be considered a part of God's eternal family? What is going on right now in your life that makes that truth extra special?

_____

_____

_____

_____

_____

Key Words from the Word

"I am fearfully and wonderfully made." *—David, Psalm 139:14*

"For we are God's handiwork, created in Christ Jesus to do good works." *—Paul, Ephesians 2:10*

"Do not fear, for I am with you; do not be dismayed, for I am your God. I will strengthen you and help you." *—God, Isaiah 41:10*

"God, who is rich in mercy, made us alive with Christ even when we were dead in transgressions." *—Paul, Ephesians 2:4–5*

> When others let you down, look up.

No Snatching

The Context: John 10:25–39

I give them eternal life, and they shall never perish;
no one will snatch them out of my hand. —Jesus, John 10:28

In the mid-1950s, General Motors displayed more at their auto shows than just cars. At one show in Miami, GM featured a display of a million one-dollar bills, as well as the Hope Diamond (the largest blue diamond in the world).

One afternoon a thunderstorm came through the city, lightning flashed, and the lights went out. Immediately, truck drivers with their flashlights rushed to the special display and formed a circle around the armed guards who were already there. The diamond and the cash were now safely guarded with two levels of security.

In John 10, Jesus described the security of His people: "I give them eternal life, and they shall never perish; no one will snatch them out of my hand" (v. 28). When we know Jesus as Savior, we're secure in His hands; we cannot lose our salvation. But there's another level of security. Jesus continued, "My Father, who has given them to me, is greater than all; no one can snatch them out of my Father's hand" (v. 29).

The Hope Diamond and the large sum of cash were quite safe with their two levels of security. How much more are we eternally safe in the hands of Jesus and His Father, the almighty God!

Jesus Moment

Think about those times when you have been fearful that your salvation was in jeopardy. How do Jesus's words in John 10 give you calmness and assurance that you are forever safe?

_____

_____

_____

_____

_____

_____

Lyrics for the Heart

My hope is built on nothing less
Than Jesus' blood and righteousness.
I dare not trust the sweetest frame,
But wholly trust in Jesus' name.
On Christ the solid Rock I stand,
All other ground is sinking sand;
All other ground is sinking sand.

"Solid Rock," Edward Mote (1797–1874)

Christ's work makes us safe;
God's Word makes us sure.

Beautiful Feet

The Context: Romans 10:14–18

How can they believe in the one of whom they have not heard? And how can they hear without someone preaching to them? —Paul, Romans 10:14

A few years ago, I met the man who had introduced me to Jesus thirty-five years earlier. Warren Wiersbe (1929–2019), former pastor of Moody Church in Chicago and Bible teacher for the Back to the Bible ministry, had preached the gospel at a Bible conference I attended. It was the first time I heard the good news of God's love for me as shown in Jesus's death on the cross. The Spirit opened my eyes and heart that night, and I received Jesus Christ as my Savior (John 1:12).

We praise the Lord for people like Warren Wiersbe, who faithfully preach the gospel and introduce others to Christ. According to the apostle Paul, they have beautiful feet: "How beautiful are the feet of those who bring good news!" (Romans 10:15).

But spreading the gospel isn't just the responsibility of Bible teachers and pastors. All who know Jesus can share on a personal level with friends, coworkers, family members, and strangers. It's our privilege and duty. Otherwise, how will people "believe in the one of whom they have not heard?" (v. 14).

Let's make our feet beautiful by bringing the good news of Jesus to others.

How will they believe in Jesus if they don't know what He did for us? And how will they hear unless someone tells them?

Jesus Moment

Just as you tell others about an important friend or relative, why not make it a point to tell about Jesus with the same excitement? Think of one or two people you know who need to hear the good news.

_____

_____

_____

_____

_____

_____

Key Words from the Word

"Therefore go and make disciples of all nations, baptizing them in the name of the Father and of the Son and of the Holy Spirit, and teaching them to obey everything I have commanded you."
—Jesus, Matthew 28:19–20

"Go into all the world and preach the gospel to all creation. Whoever believes and is baptized will be saved, but whoever does not believe will be condemned." —Jesus, Mark 16:15–16

"For I am not ashamed of the gospel, because it is the power of God that brings salvation to everyone who believes."
—Paul, Romans 1:16

"How beautiful on the mountains are the feet of one who brings good news." —Isaiah 52:7

16

Leader or Follower?

The Context: Luke 5:27–32

He said to [Levi], "Follow Me." —*Jesus, Luke 5:27 NKJV*

A close friend asked India's Mahatma Gandhi, "If you admire Christ so much, why don't you become a Christian?" It is said that he replied, "When I meet a Christian who is a follower of Christ, I may consider it."

But isn't that what a Christian is supposed to be—a follower of Christ? In his book *Following Christ*, Joe Stowell wrote, "Many of us live out our faith as though [Christ] exists to follow us. We come to believe that Christ exists to satisfy our demands. . . . This disguised form of self-serving religion sets Christ up as just one more commodity in life that will enhance and empower our dreams."

When Jesus called His disciples to follow Him, He meant that He would do the leading and directing; they would do the following (Luke 5:27). Like the disciples, we must give up our will, obey Him, and choose to "lose" our lives for Him (17:33).

At first glance, this might sound simple. But in reality, it's impossible to do on our own. Only by choosing each day to let go of our own plans and by trusting the Holy Spirit's leading can we cooperate with His work in us.

This is God's way of teaching us to become His loving, submissive followers instead of the leader.

> If you're looking for guidance,
> follow Jesus as your Guide.

Jesus Moment

Are there moments when you think, as Joe Stowell says, that it is Jesus's job to "satisfy our demands"? What are some practical ways you can turn that around and make sure you are following Jesus, not trying to lead?

_____

_____

_____

_____

_____

Thinking about Trusting the Spirit's Leading

- We often think of life's big events as moments to consider God's will (where to go to college, whom to marry, what job to take), but is it possible to allow the Holy Spirit to guide smaller decisions? As you take a look at your calendar for the next few days, what events in your life will especially need God's guidance instead of simple human wisdom?

_____

_____

- What is one ongoing area of concern that you've been dealing with on your own, and you now realize you need to follow God's leading on it?

_____

_____

Avoiding the Greener Grass

Ephesians 5:22–33

*Each one of you also must love his wife as he loves himself,
and the wife must respect her husband.* —Paul, Ephesians 5:33

Nancy Anderson says she grew lukewarm in her faith and started to believe the world's lie: "I deserve to be happy." This led to an extramarital affair that nearly ended her marriage. She wrote her book *Avoiding the Greener Grass Syndrome* to help keep her painful story of infidelity from "becoming someone else's story."

In her book, Nancy offers six action suggestions on how to build "hedges" to protect your marriage and to help make "a good marriage great":

Hear—give a listening ear to your spouse.
Encourage—build up your spouse by focusing on positive qualities.
Date—celebrate your marriage by playing and laughing together.
Guard—establish safeguards by setting clear boundaries.
Educate—study your mate to truly understand him or her.
Satisfy—meet each other's needs.

The grass on the other side of the fence may look greener, but faithfulness to God and commitment to your spouse alone bring peace of mind and satisfaction.

When you avoid the greener grass syndrome by loving and respecting your spouse, your marriage will be a picture of Christ and His church to those around you (Ephesians 5:31–32).

Jesus Moment

What do you feel the connection is between your dedication to Jesus and your relationship with your spouse? Does it seem realistic to think that staying true to Jesus will help you in staying close to your spouse?

_____

_____

_____

_____

_____

Key Words from the Word

"He who finds a wife finds what is good and receives favor from the LORD." —*Solomon, Proverbs 18:22*

"A man will leave his father and mother and be united to his wife, and the two will become one flesh." —*Paul, Ephesians 5:31*

"Marriage should be honored by all, and the marriage bed kept pure." —*Hebrews 13:4*

> Jesus Christ is the only third party in a marriage who can make it work.

18

The Fairest

The Context: Revelation 5:8–14

Worthy is the Lamb, who was slain. —*John, Revelation 5:12*

When I first became a Christian and started attending church at age eighteen, I immediately fell in love with singing the great hymns of the faith. My heart overflowed with joy and thanksgiving as we sang of God's love for us in Christ. Soon one of my favorite hymns (from the late 1600s) became "Fairest Lord Jesus." I love the simplicity of the melody and the awesomeness of the One exalted in these words:

> Fair is the sunshine, fairer still the moonlight,
> And all the twinkling starry host:
> Jesus shines brighter, Jesus shines purer
> Than all the angels heaven can boast.
> Beautiful Savior! Lord of all the nations!
> Son of God and Son of Man!
> Glory and honor, praise, adoration
> Now and forevermore be thine.

God's Son, whom we sing about in this song, came to this earth, lived a perfect life, and gave himself for us on the cross (Luke 23:33). He arose from the grave (Luke 24:6) and is now seated at God's right hand (Hebrews 1:3). One day we'll join in worship with thousands upon thousands and say: "To him who sits on the throne and to the Lamb be praise and honor and glory and power, for ever and ever!" (Revelation 5:13). Maybe we'll sing "Fairest Lord Jesus!" too.

Until then, let's allow Jesus to be "the fairest" above all in our personal lives by seeking wisdom from His Word and following in His ways.

Jesus Moment

Pause for a moment and think about what it will be like to be in that great choir in heaven—singing in unfettered joy to the glory of Jesus. What feelings does that bring to your heart and mind?

_____

_____

_____

_____

Key Words from the Word

"Those who were in the boat worshiped him, saying, 'Truly you are the Son of God.'" —*Matthew, Matthew 14:33*

"On coming to the house, [the Magi] saw the child with his mother Mary, and they bowed down and worshiped him." —*Matthew, Matthew 2:11*

"At the name of Jesus every knee should bow, in heaven and on earth and under the earth, and every tongue acknowledge that Jesus Christ is Lord, to the glory of God the Father." —*Paul, Philippians 2:10–11*

> We can never praise God enough.

"Good Buddy"

The Context: John 15:9–17

You are my friends if you do what I command.

—Jesus, John 15:14

The congregation listened intently as the pastor began to pray: "Dear heavenly Father . . . " Suddenly, he was interrupted by a voice saying, "Hey there, good buddy!"

Everyone began to laugh when they realized that the voice was coming from the organ. It was picking up the conversation of a truckdriver on his citizen's band (CB) radio! Not much was accomplished in the service that day, because the congregation continued to chuckle about the voice that made them think God was responding to their pastor and calling him His "good buddy."

Moses knew what it was like to be a friend of God—a relationship that went beyond buddies. The Lord often talked with Moses "face to face, as one speaks to a friend" (Exodus 33:11). The patriarch Abraham was also called God's friend (2 Chronicles 20:7).

But can you and I be a friend of God? In our Bible reading for today, Jesus, the supreme example of loving friendship, called His disciples friends (John 15:13, 15). He put it simply: "You are my friends if you do what I command" (v. 14).

And what does He command? That we love Him with all our heart and love others as ourselves (Mark 12:30–31). That's how we can be Jesus's friend.

Jesus Moment

Think about this concept: The Lord Jesus is not only your Savior but also your friend. Since that is true, can He be your go-to person when you need to share something important or to seek advice and help? That's an amazing idea, isn't it? What does that mean to you?

_____

_____

_____

_____

Lyrics for the Heart

What a friend we have in Jesus,
All our sins and griefs to bear!
What a privilege to carry
Everything to God in prayer . . . .

Do thy friends despise, forsake thee?
Take it to the Lord in prayer;
In His arms He'll take and shield thee,
Thou wilt find a solace there.

"What a Friend We Have in Jesus," Joseph Scriven (1819–1886)

The dearest friend on earth is but a mere shadow compared to Jesus. —*Oswald Chambers*

"There's Heaven"

The Context: Revelation 22:1–5

*They will not need the light of a lamp or the light of the sun,
for the Lord God will give them light. —John, Revelation 22:5*

When three-year-old Bree's grandpa suffered heart failure, he was taken to a local hospital where he was pronounced dead. A few weeks after the funeral, when Bree and her family drove past the hospital, she pointed to it and remarked matter-of-factly, "There's heaven." She knew her grandpa was in heaven. Since he went to the hospital on the day he died, she thought it must be heaven.

Bree's mother wrote, "We adults [have] abstract concepts of a paradise beyond even the invisible stars." Bree's childish view of heaven caused her mom to think of heaven as a real place—which helped to comfort her.

In Revelation, John gives us a glimpse of what heaven will be like. After being caught up to heaven, he saw "the river of the water of life, as clear as crystal" and "the tree of life" (22:1–2). And in that place, there will be no need for "a lamp or the light of the sun, for the Lord God will give them light" (v. 5).

Even the inspired words of John are inadequate to describe heaven, but we know it's a real place for those who have trusted Jesus as their Savior. Jesus assures us, "My Father's house has many rooms; if that were not so, would I have told you that I am going there to prepare a place for you?" (John 14:2). One day we'll be there! We will live in God's light and won't have to imagine it anymore.

Jesus Moment

There are so many things to anticipate about heaven! Go to YouTube and listen to MercyMe's song "I Can Only Imagine" to help you bask in the glory of those first moments in heaven. Any observations?

_____

_____

_____

_____

_____

_____

Lyrics for the Heart

Let us then be true and faithful,
Trusting, serving every day;
Just one glimpse of Him in glory
Will the toils of life repay.

When we all get to heaven,
What a day of rejoicing that will be!
When we all see Jesus,
We'll sing and shout the victory.

"When We All Get to Heaven," Eliza Hewitt (1851–1920)

Heaven is a prepared place
for a prepared people.

Lessons from Mom

The Context: Romans 1:8–16

I am so eager to preach the gospel also to you.
—Paul, Romans 1:15

Dementia was slowly taking Mom Cetas from us. And there was nothing my husband or I could do to keep her from slipping away.

In those difficult days, Mom taught us many lessons. She forgot how to do a number of things, but one of the things she didn't forget was how to pray. Occasionally, someone would mention a problem they were having, and she'd stop right there to pray for the person's need.

She also continued to talk to others about Jesus. Those who took care of her at the nursing home said she often asked the other residents and workers if they knew Jesus as their Savior. She wanted them to be sure that their sins were forgiven and they were going to heaven.

When I think of these qualities in Mom, I think of Romans 1. The apostle Paul remembered the people in the Roman church in his prayers "at all times" (v. 10). And he was "eager to preach the gospel" because, as he said, "I am not ashamed of the gospel, because it is the power of God that brings salvation to everyone who believes" (vv. 15–16).

As long as Mom Cetas was able, she kept looking to Jesus in prayer and telling others about Him. We all can learn from her example of boldness for Jesus and her total trust in Him.

Jesus Moment

Imagine it's your time to finish life strong. What would you want people to learn from you about living for Jesus? How can you begin now to make sure that happens?

_____

_____

_____

_____

Inspiring Words

"To be a Christian without prayer is no more possible than to be alive without breathing."
—Martin Luther, German theologian (1483–1546)

"Prayer begins where human capacity ends."
—Marian Anderson, American singer (1897–1993)

"Prayer is the greater work."
—Oswald Chambers, British Bible teacher (1874–1917)

"Any concern too small to be turned into a prayer is too small to be made into a burden."
—Corrie ten Boom, Holocaust survivor, author (1892–1983)

Talking to Christ about others gives us the passion to talk to others about Christ.

22

Valuing Others

The Context: Luke 19:1–10

The Son of Man came to seek and to save the lost.

—Jesus, Luke 19:10

As a young person, Robert had many things working against him—poverty, a broken home, a violent neighborhood. He skipped school often and was difficult to handle. But when a friend was shot to death, he considered it a wake-up call. Determined to change his life, Robert worked hard to bring his grades from failing to top marks.

Yet the school counselor did not believe in him and told him that no college would accept him. But Robert proved him wrong. He graduated from college and pursued a career in education. He chose that career because, as he says, "Teachers saw me as a nonentity"—a person of little value. He didn't want that to happen to others.

Jesus views everyone as significant. Zacchaeus was a dishonest tax collector (Luke 19:1–10). Jesus could have ignored him, but when He saw him in a tree as He walked through Jericho, He called him by name.

It's important that followers of Jesus acknowledge others as people with value. Brennan Manning writes, "A Christian who doesn't merely see but looks at another communicates to that person that he is being recognized as a human being in an impersonal world of objects."

Do the people we interact with know that we view them as valuable to us and to God?

Jesus Moment

Jesus was looking around for those He could serve, and he spotted Zacchaeus, who was "up a tree" and needed His help. How can you actively look around for others who need Jesus's touch in their lives?

_____

_____

_____

_____

_____

_____

Communicating with Jesus

Lord, you made it clear that you value all people. You were even criticized for spending time with and loving people who were not considered good enough by others. Help us to do the same. Point out to us those who are marginalized by our society, and then help us to show your love to them by talking with them and meeting their material needs where possible. Help us to avoid hanging out just with our tribe but to also spend time with people not just like us.

> Love people and not things;
> use things and not people.

23

All I Can See

He must become greater; I must become less.
—*John the Baptist, John 3:30*

Krista stood in the freezing cold, looking at the beautiful snow-encased lighthouse along the lake. As she pulled out her phone to take pictures, her glasses fogged over. She couldn't see a thing, so she decided to point her camera toward the lighthouse and snap three pictures at different angles. Looking at them later, she realized the camera had been set to take selfies. She laughed as she said, "My focus was me, me, and me. All I saw was me." Krista's photos got me thinking of a similar mistake: We can become so self-focused in life that we lose sight of the bigger picture of God's plan.

Jesus's cousin John clearly knew his focus wasn't to be on himself. Right from the start he recognized that his position or calling was to point others to Jesus, the Son of God. "Look, the Lamb of God," he said when he saw Jesus coming toward him and his followers (John 1:29). He continued, "The reason I came baptizing with water was that he might be revealed" (v. 31). When John's disciples later reported that Jesus was gaining followers, John said, "You yourselves can testify that I said, 'I am not the Messiah but am sent ahead of him.' . . . He must become greater; I must become less" (3:28–30).

May the central focus of day-to-day living be Jesus, so He becomes greater in our lives and we become less.

Jesus must increase; I must decrease.

Jesus Moment

What do you think it means to have Jesus become greater in your life?
What are some practical ways to make this happen—for His honor?

_____

_____

_____

_____

_____

Thinking about Keeping Our Focus on Jesus

- What does it really mean for us to become less in relation to
  Jesus?

_____

_____

- What are a couple of real-life ramifications of that kind of
  thinking?

_____

_____

- Who do I know who truly practices this in life? What can I
  learn by watching that person?

_____

_____

24

Is There Hope?

The Context: Matthew 28:1–10

He is not here; he has risen, just as he said.
—*An angel, Matthew 28:6*

I sat quietly at the graveside of my father, waiting for the private family burial of my mother to begin. The funeral director carried the urn that held her ashes. My heart felt numb, and my head was in a fog. How can I handle losing them both within just three months? In my grief I felt loss and loneliness and a little hopeless facing a future without them.

Then the pastor read about another graveside situation. On the first day of the week, early in the morning, some women went to Jesus's tomb, carrying spices for His body (Luke 24:1). There they were startled to find an open and empty tomb—and an angel. "Do not be afraid," he said to them (Matthew 28:5). They didn't need to be afraid of the empty tomb or of the angel, because he had good news for them.

Hope stirred when I heard the next words: "He is not here; he has risen, just as he said" (v. 6). Because Jesus had come back to life, death had been conquered! Jesus reminded His followers just a few days before His death: "Because I live, you also will live" (John 14:19).

Even though we grieve at the loss of our loved ones, we find hope through the resurrection of Jesus and His promise that there is life after death.

Jesus Moment

You grieve at the graveside, and rightly so. But because Jesus overpowered death, you know that the soul of your believing loved one is now in Jesus's presence. You can cling to that comfort when hope seems lost. How do you react to that truth?

_____

_____

_____

_____

_____

Lyrics for the Heart

Jesus paid it all,
All to Him I owe;
Sin had left a crimson stain,
He washed it white as snow.

And when, before the throne,
I stand in Him complete,
"Jesus died my soul to save,"
My lips shall still repeat.

"Jesus Paid It All," Elvina M. Hall (1818–1889)

Because He lives, we live.

Fake Family

The Context: Matthew 15:1–9

These people honor me with their lips,
but their hearts are far from me. —Jesus, Matthew 15:8

A builder in California came up with an innovative idea to sell his houses. He thinks that a good way to make a house more appealing is to have a family there when showing the house. So he hires actors to play happy families in his company's model homes. Would-be buyers can ask them questions about the house. Each fake family cooks, watches television, and plays games while house-hunters wander through.

That type of faking may not do any harm, but think about the sham of the religious leaders in Jesus's day (Matthew 15:1–9). They pretended to love God and piously made up a long list of rules that they and others were to obey. But this was only to make themselves look good. They even considered their rules to be just as important as the Law that came directly from the Lord (vv. 5–6). Jesus called them "hypocrites" (v. 7). He said their words sounded as if they honored God, but their hearts told another story—they were far from Him (v. 8).

That kind of pretending goes on today as well. We look like good Christians on the outside because we go to church faithfully, follow some rules legalistically, and use the right words. It is possible to say we love Jesus while our hearts are far from Him. God wants us to be real.

A false front can disguise a true faith.

Jesus Moment

Is it possible you are doing some things for show? In what ways? This is a "between me and Jesus" thing, so talk about it with Him and ask Him for help to be real in your relationship with Him.

_____

_____

_____

_____

_____

Thinking about Being a Good Christian

- The last paragraph of the article mentions three things we often associate with "good Christians." Indeed, going to church, obeying scriptural standards, and speaking with kindness and civility are important. But what is more important than those as we consider our walk with God?

_____

_____

- Why do we love God, anyway? Is it anything we have done that caused this relationship? Once we recognize that it is all His doing and none of ours, how does that change our relationship with Him?

_____

_____

Scaredy-Bear

The Context: Matthew 6:25–34

Do not worry. —Jesus, Matthew 6:25

Jack, a fifteen-pound orange and white cat, took seriously his job of guarding his owners' backyard in New Jersey. He often scared away small animal intruders, but the owners were surprised when one day they found him sitting at the base of a tall tree, looking up at a large black bear.

Jack hissed at the bear when it had wandered into the yard from the nearby woods. The scared bear quickly climbed up a tree. How could a big black bear be afraid of a little kitty? What was he thinking!

Even more absurd are our thoughts of worry and fear when we consider that we have a powerful and good God who cares for us. Jesus told His disciples, "Do not worry" (Matthew 6:25, 31, 34). He said we don't have to be fearful or worried because our heavenly Father knows our needs, and we are valued by Him (vv. 26, 32). He is perfectly willing and able to meet our needs.

When something concerns us, what's our perspective? It's not *what we see* but *how we see it* that reveals our hearts. If we learn to look at life through the lens of our powerful and good God, we'll trust Him instead of fearfully worrying. When our perspective is right, we can see God and His faithful provision.

Jesus Moment

What is the harmless house cat that is scaring you today? How does that problem look next to Jesus and His willingness to carry your burdens? Pretty puny, probably. Tell Jesus what you fear, and ask Him to help you trust Him.

_____

_____

_____

_____

_____

Inspiring Words

"Worry implies that we don't quite trust [that] God is big enough."
—Francis Chan, American author, pastor

"Worry does not empty tomorrow of its sorrows; it empties today of its strength." —Corrie ten Boom, Holocaust survivor, author (1892–1983)

"Worry is interest paid on trouble before it is due."
—William R. Inge, British clergyman (1860–1954)

> Worry is a burden that God never meant for us to bear.

27

No More Mowing

The Context: Luke 10:38–42

Martha, . . . few things are needed —
or indeed only one. —Jesus, Luke 10:41–42

The mayor of a small town in Kentucky stopped mowing his lawn. He put up a sign on his property that reads: "There are more important things in life than tall grass."

He said that he has several reasons for not cutting the grass, one of which is his wife's death from cancer. That loss caused him to reflect on the priorities of life. He also says he enjoys sitting in the evenings and observing the wildflowers, squirrels, and birds that come to his yard. A member of the city council remarked, "If he likes it like that, it's fine. I kind of feel like maybe he is right. Maybe there are more important things than mowing grass."

The mayor gives us some food for thought about priorities. What we do with our time shows what we feel is important. In Luke 10:38–42, we read that when Jesus came to visit, Martha was "distracted by all the preparations" (Luke 10:40). Mary, however, took the time to sit "at the Lord's feet" and listen to His teaching (v. 39). Of the few things that needed to be done, this was the "only one" that was essential (v. 42).

Sometimes important responsibilities like washing dishes, mowing the lawn, or working extra hours on a project need to wait so we can spend time with the Lord or family or friends. That may be what's more important.

Jesus Moment

Is sitting at Jesus's feet a priority? You do that when you pray and meditate on God's Word. Without neglecting essential activities, how can you begin to do the "one thing" that is needed?

_____

_____

_____

_____

_____

_____

Lyrics for the Heart

What a friend we have in Jesus,
All our sins and griefs to bear!
What a privilege to carry
Everything to God in prayer!

Are we weak and heavy laden,
Cumbered with a load of care?
Precious Savior, still our refuge—
Take it to the Lord in prayer.

"What a Friend We Have in Jesus," Joseph Scriven (1819–1886)

Jesus wants us to walk with Him
and focus on who He is.

28

Our Living Hope

The Context: John 6:39–54

*God . . . has given us new birth into a living hope through
the resurrection of Jesus Christ from the dead. —Peter, 1 Peter 1:3*

The morning after my mother died, I was reading the Bible and talking to
the Lord about my sadness. The Bible in One Year reading for that day was
John 6.

When I came to verse 39, the Lord whispered comfort to my sad heart
through these words: "This is the will of the Father who sent Me, that of
all He has given Me I should lose nothing, but should raise it up at the last
day" (NKJV). Mom's spirit was with the Lord already, but I knew that one
day she would be raised and given a new body.

As I continued reading, I noticed three other times in John 6 that Jesus
said He will raise His people from the dead at the last day. He was repeat-
ing this truth to those who were listening long ago as well as to my heart
that day.

Our hope of resurrection will be realized when Jesus returns. "In a flash,
in the twinkling of an eye, at the last trumpet. For the trumpet will sound,
and the dead will be raised imperishable, and we will be changed" (1 Corinthians 15:52). After the resurrection, believers in Jesus will receive their
new bodies and rewards for their faithful service (1 Corinthians 3:12–15;
2 Corinthians 5:9–11).

The resurrection is the living hope of the Christian. Do you have that
hope?

Jesus Moment

Jesus Christ will one day return to this earth, Scripture says. What new hope does that give you as you consider the ups and downs of life?

_____

_____

_____

_____

Lyrics for the Heart

Let us labor for the Master
From the dawn till setting sun,
Let us talk of all His wondrous love and care;
Then when all of life is over,
And our work on earth is done,
And the roll is called up yonder,
I'll be there.

"When the Roll Is Called Up Yonder," James Black (1856–1938)

> The risen Christ will come from heaven
> to take His own to heaven.

29

Will Work for Friends

The Context: Acts 4:32–37

There were no needy persons among them.
—Luke, Acts 4:34

Six friends formed a home-repair club in Minneapolis, Minnesota. They met one Saturday a month at one of their homes to work on projects that could not be tackled alone. Having helped one another for twenty years, they said this effort bonded them together like one big family. A similar group was formed in Snohomish, Washington. Their motto is "Will Work for Friends."

The concern of these groups for their friends reminds me of the early church (Acts 4:32–37). During this time of great persecution of believers, they especially needed the support of one another. Some people voluntarily sold their land and houses and brought the proceeds to the apostles, and "it was distributed to anyone who had need" (v. 35). They were "one in heart" and "shared everything they had" (v. 32).

As followers of Christ today, we too need the spiritual support and encouragement of one another. We may be struggling with a decision about how to serve the Lord. Maybe we're concerned about a problem at work. Or perhaps we're unsure of how to discipline a rebellious child. These are good opportunities to enlist the advice and prayer of fellow Christians.

Through love, let's serve one another—physically and spiritually—in the family of God (Galatians 5:13).

Jesus Moment

The church is a natural place for these kinds of activities to happen. There doesn't have to be a formal organization for fellow believers to be Jesus to each other by helping friends make it through life. What needs do you see?

_____

_____

_____

_____

_____

Action Steps

We can be either a receiver of good deeds from others or a doer of good deeds for others. Let's look at both.

- If you are one who loves doing good things for other people, what opportunities do you feel you are most equipped by God to take care of?

_____

_____

- List three people you know who need that kind of helpful intervention. What do you think you might be able to do for each?

_____

_____

- Now think about your own needs. What help could you use spiritually or physically? Who in your church or Bible study group could possibly come to your aid? Do you feel comfortable asking for help?

_____

_____

Christians stand strong when they stand together.

30

The Pretender

The Context: Genesis 27:19–33

Confess your sins to each other and pray for each other so that you may be healed. —James, James 5:16

When a female server in an Ohio restaurant asked to see a customer's driver's license, she was shocked when she saw the photo on the ID. It was her own picture! The server had lost her driver's license a month earlier, and this young woman was using it so she'd have "proof" she was old enough to drink alcohol. The police were called, and the customer was arrested for identity theft. Trying to gain what she wanted, she pretended to be someone she wasn't.

Jacob, in the Old Testament, did some pretending too. With his mother Rebekah's help, he fooled his father into believing he was his brother Esau so he could gain the blessing meant for the oldest son (Genesis 27). Jacob did get caught after his deceitful act, but it was too late for Esau to receive the blessing.

Pretending goes on in our churches today. Some people put on a false front. They use the right "Christian" words, post Bible verses on Facebook, and even pray before meals. They pretend they "have it all together" in order to gain the approval of others. But inside they're struggling with brokenness, guilt, doubt, or an addiction or other persistent sin. They need a fresh view of Jesus's forgiveness and grace.

God placed us in a body of believers to support one another. Admit that you aren't perfect. Then seek the counsel of a godly brother or sister in Christ.

Jesus Moment

It is easy to be more concerned about appearances than it is to repair the real picture. How can your relationship with Jesus lift you out of being a pretender and push you toward confession and a clean slate?

_____

_____

_____

_____

_____

Thinking about Pretending

- What do you pretend about most when it comes to faith matters? Do you think God is fooled? What is the best way to reenter reality regarding this?

_____

_____

- What signal does it send to nonbelievers if they notice that we behave inconsistently? For instance, if our neighbor sees us going to church but hears us yelling at our children—what good are we doing?

_____

_____

- What Bible character do you see as being the most genuine (other than Jesus, of course)? What real lessons can he or she teach us?

_____

_____

Walking in the light of truth will help keep us out of life's darkest corners.

31

Rescued!

The Context: Ephesians 2:1–10

God, who is rich in mercy, made us alive with Christ.
—Paul, Ephesians 2:4–5

Lauren nervously yet excitedly hopped into a one-person kayak for a white-water rafting experience. After strapping herself in, she headed down the river with a group of kayakers and guides.

Lauren became even more nervous when she laid eyes on the falls ahead. Suddenly, as the kayak tossed and turned in the white water, it flipped over. She had been instructed on how to get out quickly if this were to happen. But she became disoriented as she hung upside down in the water and couldn't find the release bar to get out. She knew she couldn't hold her breath much longer and thought she would soon be in the Lord's presence. Then help came just in time and she was saved. Lauren was very grateful for her rescue from physical death.

An even greater rescue has been provided for us! Rescue from spiritual death has come in the person of Jesus Christ. While we were drowning in sin, God sent His Son Jesus to bring life through His own death and resurrection (Romans 5:8; Ephesians 2:5). He did so because He is "rich in mercy" and because of "his great love" (Ephesians 2:4).

Out of gratefulness, we can help others by telling them of the Rescuer they so desperately need.

> Those who have been rescued need to be ready and willing to help in the rescue of others.

Jesus Moment

Lauren knew she needed to be rescued. However, many people don't know they need rescue from the penalty of their sin. How can you gently but compassionately let an unsaved friend or relative know he or she *must* be rescued by Jesus?

_____

_____

_____

_____

_____

Lyrics for the Heart

Rescue the perishing,
Care for the dying,
Snatch them in pity from sin and the grave;
Weep o'er the erring one,
Lift up the fallen,
Tell them of Jesus, the mighty to save.

Rescue the perishing,
Care for the dying,
Jesus is merciful,
Jesus will save.

"Rescue the Perishing," Fanny Crosby (1820–1915)

32

Instant Access

The Context: Hebrews 10:19–23

Let us draw near to God with a sincere heart and with
the full assurance that faith brings. —author, Hebrews 10:22

Pastor Rich McCarrell explained to his young son how his secretary screened his phone calls at the church office. He said, "If your mom calls me and I'm busy, the church secretary will tell her what I'm doing, and then Mom will decide if I should be interrupted or if she should leave a message."

Then he said to his son, "If you call me, you'll be put right through. I want you to know that you can call me anytime, because you're my son."

A few days later, the church secretary put a call through to the pastor from his son. Pastor McCarrell said hello and asked what he could do for his son. He replied, "Nothing, Dad. I just wanted to make sure I could actually get through to you that easily."

Instant access. That is exactly what we have with our Father in heaven. There's no secretary to screen His calls. No need for a decision on whether or not we should bother Him. No need to leave a message so He can get back to us later. The psalmist reminds us, "The eyes of the LORD are on the righteous, and his ears are attentive to their cry" (Psalm 34:15).

Jesus opened the way to the Father by His death and resurrection—giving us boldness and confidence as we draw near to our Father (Hebrews 4:16).

Jesus Moment

What situation has your attention currently? Take a moment right now and throughout your day to call on your heavenly Father. He's always ready to listen to your prayer.

_____

_____

_____

_____

_____

_____

Key Words from the Word

"Call to me and I will answer you and tell you great and unsearchable things you do not know." —*God, Jeremiah 33:3*

"The righteous cry out, and the Lord hears them; he delivers them from all their troubles." —*David, Psalm 34:17*

"The Lord is near to all who call on him, to all who call on him in truth." —*David, Psalm 145:18*

Through prayer we have instant access
to our Father in heaven.

33

Will I Have to Tell?

The Context: 2 Corinthians 5:12–21

Therefore, if anyone is in Christ, the new creation has come:
The old has gone, the new is here! —Paul, 2 Corinthians 5:17

Jim was explaining the gospel of Jesus to Kerri. He told her she was separated from a holy God because of her sin and that Jesus Christ had died and risen for her salvation. She mentioned repeatedly her one reason not to believe: "But if I do receive Him, I won't have to tell other people about it, will I? I don't want to do that." She said that didn't fit her personality; she didn't want to have to tell others about Jesus.

Jim explained that promising to witness about Jesus is not a requirement before trusting Him. But he also said that once she came to know the Lord as Savior, Kerri would become His ambassador to the world (2 Corinthians 5:20).

After talking a little longer, Kerri acknowledged her need for salvation through Christ. She went home excited and at peace. Then a funny thing happened—within twenty-four hours she told three people about what God had done in her life.

Because we have been reconciled to God through Jesus, we now have "the ministry of reconciliation," according to the apostle Paul (v. 18). We are Jesus's ambassadors, and therefore we implore people "on Christ's behalf: Be reconciled to God" (v. 20).

When we're thankful, we want to share what Jesus has done.

Jesus Moment

Is it in your nature to be able to tell others about Jesus? If so, ask God to help you find friends to share with. If not, ask God for the courage you need to say a word "on Christ's behalf" to someone who doesn't know Him. Who might that be?

_____

_____

_____

_____

_____

Inspiring Words

"Yes, let God be the judge. Your job today is to be a witness."
—*Warren Wiersbe, American Bible teacher (1929–2019)*

"People pay attention when they see that God actually changes persons and sets them free." —*Jim Cymbala, American pastor*

"Let others report bad news; we'll share the good news."
—*Woodrow Kroll, American Bible teacher*

"Being an extrovert isn't essential to evangelism—obedience and love are." —*Becky Pippert, American author and speaker*

> There is no better news than the gospel—
> spread the word!

34

Unanswered

The Context: Luke 18:1–8

*Jesus told his disciples a parable to show them
that they should always pray and not give up. —Luke, Luke 18:1*

One of my biggest struggles is waiting for answers to prayer. Maybe you
can relate. You ask God to rescue a friend from addiction, to grant salvation to a loved one, to heal a sick child, to mend a relationship. All these
things you think must be God's will. For years you pray. But you hear
nothing back from Him, and you see no results.

You remind the Lord that He's powerful. That your request is a good
thing. You plead. You wait. You doubt—maybe He doesn't hear you, or
maybe He isn't so powerful after all. You quit asking—for days or months.
You feel guilty about doubting. You remember that God wants you to take
your needs to Him, so you tell Him your requests again.

We may sometimes feel we're like the persistent widow in Jesus's parable
recorded in Luke 18. She keeps coming to the judge, badgering him and
trying to wear him down so he'll give in. But we know that God is kinder
and more powerful than the judge in the parable. We trust Him, for He
is good and wise and sovereign. We remember that Jesus said we "should
always pray and not give up" (v. 1).

So we ask Him, "Summon your power, God; show us your strength,
our God, as you have done before" (Psalm 68:28). And then we trust Him
again . . . and wait.

Jesus Moment

Think about Jesus's words: "Always pray." And "not give up." No exceptions, apparently. No apologies. Just tell Him. And tell Him again. And again. Do. Not. Give. Up. How can this thinking change your prayer life?

_____

_____

_____

_____

Thinking about Unanswered Prayer

- What are some prayers that I just can't seem to get answers for?

_____

_____

- How does this affect my faith in God's ability to answer my prayer?

_____

_____

- How might Jesus be saying back to me, "Don't give up"?

_____

_____

- What is my response to that possibility?

_____

_____

> Delay is not denial, so keep praying.

35

Like Jesus

The Context: 1 John 2:5–11

*He who says he abides in [Jesus] ought himself
also to walk just as He walked. —John, 1 John 2:6 NKJV*

During a children's church service, the teacher talked about the first of the Ten Commandments: "You shall have no other gods before me" (Exodus 20:3). She suggested some ways for the kids to keep this command. She said, "Nothing should come before God—not candy, not schoolwork, not video games." She told them that putting God first meant that time with Him reading the Bible and praying should come before anything else.

An older child in the group responded with a thought-provoking question. She asked if being a Christian was about keeping rules or if instead God wanted to be involved in all areas of our life.

Sometimes we make the mistake of viewing the Bible as a list of rules. Certainly, obeying God (John 14:21) is important but not because we must measure up to a list. Jesus and the Father had a loving relationship. When we have a relationship with God, we desire to get to know Him. We spend time with Him and obey Him so we can become more like Jesus. John said, "He who says he abides in [Jesus] ought himself also to walk just as He walked" (1 John 2:6 NKJV). Jesus is the example we can follow.

When we want to understand how to love, or how to be humble, or how to have faith, or even how to set our priorities, we can look at Jesus. Our goal is not just to follow rules but to follow Jesus's heart.

Jesus Moment

What are three areas of life in which you want to be like Jesus? For instance, in His willingness to forgive. Or in His compassion for others. What are some ways in these and other areas to "walk just as He walked"?

_____

_____

_____

_____

_____

_____

Communicating with Jesus

Can I ask you, Lord, to give me daily guidance as I seek to live as you want me to live? Please help me drop from my life all activities that push me away from you. And when I interact with those who don't know you or are antagonistic toward you, help me to know how to respond. Help me to show compassion for others, as you did. Please allow me the humble reality of walking as you would have me walk through life.

Jesus calls us to follow Him.

36

The Best Life

The Context: John 1:35–42

The first thing Andrew did was to find his brother Simon and tell him, "We have found the Messiah." —John, John 1:41

A few years ago, I had to travel to Florida on business. On my flight home to Michigan, I was pleasantly surprised to find that I had a seat with lots of leg room. It felt so good not to be scrunched into a small area. Plus, I had an empty seat beside me! The makings of a good nap.

Then I remembered those around me in their not-as-comfortable seats. I invited several others I knew to join me in a better spot but was surprised they all wanted to stay in their own seats for various reasons: They either didn't want to be inconvenienced with a move or felt fine where they were.

As believers in Christ, we have a much more significant invitation to extend: We've received a new life of faith in Jesus, and we want others to experience it too. Some will want to do so and others won't. In John 1:40 we read that Andrew had begun to follow Jesus. The first thing Andrew did was to find his brother Simon and invite him to meet Jesus, the Messiah, too (v. 41). Jesus offered them a wonderful new life of knowing Him and enjoying His promises: His forgiveness (Ephesians 1:7), continual presence (Hebrews 13:5), hope (Romans 15:13), peace (John 14:27), and a forever future in His presence (1 Thessalonians 4:17).

Won't you join in? Jesus gives the best life.

> If you want someone to know what Christ will do for her, let her see what Christ has done for you.

Jesus Moment

If you are a follower of Jesus, what makes it "the best life"? Can you list several things that you are grateful Jesus provides for you? Take a moment and thank Him for who He is and all He has done for you.

_____

_____

_____

_____

_____

Thinking about the Best Life

- If you are a follower of Jesus Christ, you have found hope and joy and comfort in the salvation He provides. Why do you think Christianity is viewed by so many people in a negative light?

_____

_____

- If someone were to confront you and say, "Okay, tell me what is so great about being a Christian," what do you think you would tell that person?

_____

_____

- Are you ever tempted to look over the landscape of our culture and wonder what it would be like to be on the other side? What keeps you following Jesus and not drifting away?

_____

_____

37

You Can Beat It!

The Context: Matthew 28:1–10

Where, O death, is your sting?
—*Paul quoting Hosea, 1 Corinthians 15:55*

The radio ad for an upcoming seminar sounded intriguing. The announcer said, "You can beat death—for good! Attend my seminar and I'll show you how." I wondered for a few moments what the speaker would claim could beat death and what his suggestions might be. Perhaps something about diet or exercise or freezing our bodies? After listening a little longer, though, I realized he had said, "You can beat *debt*—for good."

That was okay, because had I already learned how to beat death.

We can beat *death* because Jesus paid our *debt* (1 Corinthians 15:55–57). Our debt of sin meant separation from God forever, but Jesus willingly gave up His life and was crucified on a cross to pay what we owed. As Mary Magdalene and another Mary went to the tomb on the third day to anoint His body, an angel told them: "He is not here; he has risen, just as he said" (Matthew 28:6). With great joy they ran to bring His disciples the word. On their way, Jesus met them and said, "Rejoice!" (v. 9 NKJV). Jesus had risen, and His followers had reason for rejoicing.

Jesus has removed the sting of death (1 Corinthians 15:55). Now we too have victory by believing in Jesus's death and resurrection for us. Through Jesus's perfect work, we can beat death—for good!

Jesus Moment

When you think of the idea of death, what most bothers you? Have you had your debt paid through faith in Jesus? And if you have, has that given you a calm assurance about facing death?

_____

_____

_____

_____

_____

_____

Lyrics for the Heart

Christ the Lord is risen today, Alleluia!
Earth and heaven in chorus say, Alleluia!
Raise your joys and triumphs high, Alleluia!
Sing, ye heavens, and earth reply, Alleluia!
Love's redeeming work is done, Alleluia!
Fought the fight, the battle won, Alleluia!
Death in vain forbids him rise, Alleluia!
Christ has opened paradise, Alleluia!

"Christ the Lord Is Risen Today," Charles Wesley (1707–1788)

We owed a debt we couldn't pay;
Jesus paid a debt He didn't owe.

38

Creating Your Life

The Context: Mark 10:35–45

Whoever wants to be first must be slave of all.

—Jesus, Mark 10:44

The advice that I read in a self-help book sounded good at first: Do only what you're great at because that's when you'll feel most fulfilled. The author was trying to help readers create the kind of life they wanted. But the more I thought about it, the less I liked it. I don't know about you, but if I did only what I was great at, I wouldn't accomplish much!

In Mark 10, we read about two disciples, James and John, who had some plans for the kind of life they wanted for themselves someday. They asked to be at Jesus's right and left hand in His kingdom (v. 37). The other ten disciples were "greatly displeased" with them for asking (v. 41 NKJV). (Possibly because that was the kind of position they wanted for themselves!)

But Jesus used the opportunity to teach His followers about another kind of life—one of serving others. He said, "Whoever wants to become great among you must be your servant, and whoever wants to be first must be slave of all" (vv. 43–44). It appears that service for others is not some kind of punishment; it is God's design for us.

Even Jesus, the Son of God, "did not come to be served, but to serve" (v. 45). As we look at Christ's example and depend on the Holy Spirit's help, we too can be servants. And maybe we can even become great at it.

Jesus Moment

How does the idea of being a servant strike you? You might think, I already run the kids everywhere, have a job, and manage a household. What else is there? It might be all that's needed is an attitude of serving Jesus with joy.

_____

_____

_____

_____

_____

Key Words from the Word

"For who is greater, the one who is at the table or the one who serves? Is it not the one who is at the table? But I am among you as one who serves." —Jesus, Luke 22:27

"Whoever serves me must follow me; and where I am, my servant also will be. My Father will honor the one who serves me." —Jesus, John 12:26

"In humility value others above yourselves, not looking to your own interests but each of you to the interests of the others." —Paul, Philippians 2:3–4

Great occasions for serving God come seldom, but little ones surround us daily.

39

Not Interested in Religion

The Context: John 5:18, 37–47

How often I have longed to gather your children together, as a hen gathers her chicks under her wings, and you were not willing. —Jesus, Matthew 23:37

A radio ad for a church caught my attention: "Because you've heard about Christianity, you might not be interested in religion. Well, it might surprise you—Jesus wasn't interested in religion either. But He was big on relationship and teaching us to love one another." It continued, "You may not like everything about our church, but we offer authentic relationship, and we're learning to love God and each other. You're welcome to visit."

This church may have overstated things about Jesus and religion, because Scripture does speak of true religion in James 1:27 as helpful deeds toward others. But Jesus did have difficulties with religious people of His day. He said the Pharisees, guided by tradition and rules not by love for the Lord, "on the outside . . . [appear] as righteous but on inside [they] are full of hypocrisy and wickedness" (Matthew 23:28). They didn't have the love of God in their hearts (John 5:42). Jesus wanted relationship with them, but they refused "to come to [him]" (v. 40).

If being "religious" means following a set of rules so we can look good—instead of enjoying a relationship with the Savior—Jesus isn't interested. He offers forgiveness and love to all who want an intimate relationship with Him.

> There is a longing in every heart
> that only Jesus can satisfy.

Jesus Moment

Do others see you as "religious" or "in relationship with Jesus"? In many cases, friends who don't understand the gospel just see us as being "religious." How can you show them Jesus and not religion?

_____

_____

_____

_____

Thinking about Religion

People often think of religion as man reaching up to God. However, that formula never works. God reached down to man in the person of Jesus.

- What are some things "religious" people do that makes them feel better but does not get them any closer to God?

_____

_____

- The world likes to refer to people who love God as religious because that's a category everyone fits into from time to time. How is having a relationship with Jesus Christ—through faith in His death, burial, and resurrection—different from the general view people have of religion?

_____

_____

40

Two Men

The Context: John 11:30–37

He was deeply moved in spirit
and troubled. . . . Jesus wept. —*John, John 11:33, 35*

Two men were killed in our city on the same day. The first, a police officer, was shot while trying to help a family. The other was a homeless man who was shot while drinking with friends early that day.

The whole city grieved for the police officer. He was a fine young man who cared for others and was loved by the neighborhood he served. A few homeless people grieved for the friend they loved and lost.

I think the Lord grieved with them all.

When Jesus saw Mary and Martha and their friends weeping over the death of Lazarus, "He was deeply moved in spirit and troubled" (John 11:33). He loved Lazarus and his sisters. Even though He knew He would soon be raising Lazarus from the dead, He wept with them (v. 35). Some Bible scholars think that part of the reason for Jesus's weeping may also have been over death itself and the pain and sadness it causes in people's hearts.

Loss is a part of life. But because Jesus is "the resurrection and the life" (v. 25), those who believe in Him will one day experience an end of all death and sorrow. In the meantime, He weeps with us over our losses and asks us to "mourn with those who mourn" (Romans 12:15).

Jesus Moment

Mourning with others is hard work. It is difficult to know just what to do. Notice that we aren't told Jesus said anything profound to Mary. He just grieved. People need you to be with them and share their sorrow—to show both empathy and sympathy in their painful moments.

_____

_____

_____

_____

_____

_____

Communicating with Jesus

Dear Jesus, help me learn from you what compassion is all about. You cared deeply and passionately about all kinds of people— from the disabled to the sinful to the souls who were lost. Help me to hold out a hand of help to everyone I see who needs the love you demonstrated and the love you have put in my heart through your gift of salvation. Help my compassion for others to mirror yours.

> Compassion helps to heal the hurts of others.

41

Jesus Loves You

The Context: John 19:17–24

Carrying his own cross, he went out to the place of the Skull. . . .
There they crucified him. —John, John 19:17–18

It was a bit unusual, but three times in one day I heard the same song.

In the early afternoon, I attended a hymn sing at a home for the elderly. As part of her prayer at the end of our time together, Willie, one of the residents, said, "Sing with me, 'Jesus Loves Me.'" In the evening, I attended a gathering with young people who sang it while pounding out the beat with their hands and feet. Later that night, I received a text message with an audio recording of my two-and-a-half-year-old grandniece with a sweet little voice, singing, "I am weak, but He is strong." People in their nineties, teenagers, and a toddler all sang that song that day.

After hearing that simple song three times, I began to think God might be telling me something. Actually, He gave all of us this message long ago: "I love you." We read in John 19 that He allowed people to put a crown of thorns on His head, mock Him, strike Him, strip Him, and crucify Him (vv. 1–6). He had the power to stop them, but He said very little (v. 11). He did it all for love's sake to pay for our sins and to rescue us from punishment.

How much does God love you? Jesus spread out His arms and was nailed to the cross for you. He died for you, then rose again. That's a precious fact for you and me—whether we are young or old.

Jesus Moment

Think of how comforting and encouraging it is to know that a person—a friend, a spouse, a son or daughter, a parent—loves you. Now think of this: Jesus, who was God in the flesh and who is now seated at God's right hand in heaven, loves you as well. Overwhelming, isn't it! What are some thoughts that go through your head as you contemplate that love?

_____

_____

_____

_____

_____

Inspiring Words

"The truest measure of God's love is that He loves without measure!" —*Bernard of Clairvaux, French abbot (1090–1153)*

"God proved His love on the cross. When Christ hung, and bled, and died, it was God saying to the world, 'I love you.'" —*Billy Graham, American evangelist (1918–2018)*

"The shape of true love isn't a diamond. It's a cross." —*Alicia Bruxvoort, American author*

Christ's death is the measure of God's love for you.

42

"If You Are Willing"

Matthew 8:1–4

"Lord, if you are willing, you can make me clean."
—A leper, Matthew 8:2

Molly wanted her dad's help, but she was afraid to ask. She knew that when he was working at his computer, he didn't want to be interrupted. *He might get upset at me*, she thought, so she didn't ask him.

We need not have such fears when we think about going to Jesus with our thoughts, prayers, and concerns. In Matthew 8:1–4, we read about a leper who didn't hesitate to interrupt Jesus with his needs. His disease made him desperate—he had been ostracized from society and was in emotional distress. Jesus was busy with "large crowds" (v. 1), but the leper made his way through the crowd to talk with Jesus.

Matthew's gospel says that the leper came and "worshiped Him" (v. 2 NKJV). He approached Jesus in worship, with trust in His power, and with humility, acknowledging that the choice to help belonged to Jesus. He said, "Lord, if you are willing, you can make me clean" (v. 2). In compassion, Jesus touched him (leprosy had made him "untouchable" by the standards of Jewish law), and he was cleansed immediately.

Like the leper, we don't need to hesitate to approach Jesus with our desire for His help. As we go to Him in humility and worship, we can trust that He will make the best choices for us.

Jesus Moment

Jesus is never too busy for you to approach Him in prayer. Why not pause right now and have a good, long talk with Him—praising Him for who He is and then sharing your burdens with Him (1 Peter 5:7).

_____

_____

_____

_____

Communicating with Jesus

You taught us, Lord, to pray to your Father in heaven and hallow His name. So, please accept my praise and adoration to God the Father, God the Son, and God the Holy Spirit. May today be one of dedication to your service. Guide me in what I say and do today. Help me to love sacrificially and to comfort those in need while serving you unconditionally. Thank you in advance for your provisions for this day and giving me spiritual life through the cross.

> "Let us . . . come boldly to the throne of grace,
> that we may obtain mercy." —*Hebrews 4:16 NKJV*

43

More Than Waiting

The Context: Acts 1:1–11

In a little while you will see me no more, and then after a little while you will see me. . . . Because I am going to the Father. —Jesus, John 16:16–17

I don't know how it works where you live, but when I have to call for a repair for one of my appliances, the company says something like, "The repairman will be there between 1:00 p.m. and 5:00 p.m." Since I don't know when the repair person will actually arrive, all I can do is wait.

Jesus told His followers that He would soon be leaving them, and they would need to wait for His return in "a little while" (John 16:16). After His resurrection, they saw Him again, and they hoped He would be establishing His kingdom on earth at that time. But He told them, "It is not for you to know the times or dates the Father has set by his own authority" (Acts 1:7). They would have to wait even longer.

But they were to do more than wait. Jesus told His followers that they were to "be my witnesses in Jerusalem, and in all Judea and Samaria, and to the ends of the earth" (v. 8). And He gave them the Holy Spirit to empower them to do this.

We still wait for Jesus's return. And while we do, it's our delight, in the Holy Spirit's power, to tell and show others who Jesus is, what He has done for all of us through His death and resurrection, and that He has promised to return.

Wait and witness till Jesus returns.

Jesus Moment

Believers wait for Jesus's return with anticipation—like waiting for a loved one who has gone on a long trip. How does it change your perspective on life to realize that Jesus could return at any time?

_____

_____

_____

_____

Action Steps

As you consider the imminent return of Jesus, what should you be thinking about in preparation? Here are some ideas:

- Others: Is there anyone you feel you should introduce to Jesus?

_____

_____

- Yourself: If you were getting ready for someone to come to your house, what would you do? If you are getting ready for Jesus to return, what similar activities are needed?

_____

_____

- Jesus: In what ways are you ready to meet Him? In what ways are you not quite ready?

_____

_____

44

Too Much for Me

The Context: Matthew 26:36–46

My Father, if it is possible,
may this cup be taken from me. —Jesus, *Matthew 26:39*

"God never gives us more than we can handle," someone said to a father whose five-year-old son had just lost his battle with cancer. These words, which were intended to encourage him, instead depressed him and caused him to wonder why he wasn't "handling" the loss of his boy very well. The pain was so much to bear that he could hardly even breathe. He knew his grief was too much for him and that he desperately needed God to hold him tight.

The verse that some use to support the statement "God never gives us more than we can handle" is 1 Corinthians 10:13: "When you are tempted, he will also provide a way out so that you can endure it." But the context of these words is temptation, not suffering. We can choose the way out of temptation that God provides, but we can't choose a way out of suffering.

Jesus himself wanted a way out of His upcoming suffering when He prayed, "My soul is overwhelmed with sorrow to the point of death. . . . My Father, if it is possible, may this cup be taken from me" (Matthew 26:38–39). Yet He willingly went through this for our salvation.

When life seems too much to bear, that's when we throw ourselves on God's mercy, and He holds on to us.

Jesus Moment

Sometimes the pain is too great to bear. But you are not without resource. You have a Savior who understands sorrow and pain, and He told us to unload our burdens onto His shoulders. Jesus will help carry you through your painful circumstances. Can you recall some times He has done that for you?

_____

_____

_____

_____

_____

Action Steps

Here are some books that might help if you have gone through a "pain too great to bear."

- *A Grief Observed*, C. S. Lewis, HarperCollins Publishers
- *Beyond the Valley*, Dave Branon, Our Daily Bread Publishing
- *Walking with God through Pain and Suffering*, Timothy Keller, Penguin Publishing
- *Where Is God When It Hurts?* Philip Yancey, Zondervan

> With God behind you and His arms beneath you, you can face whatever lies ahead.

45

The Main Event

The Context: Luke 10:38–42

One thing is needed, and Mary has chosen that good part.
—Jesus, Luke 10:42 NKJV

While watching a fireworks display during a celebration in my city, I became distracted. Off to the right and the left of the main event, smaller fireworks occasionally popped up in the sky. They were good, but watching them caused me to miss parts of the more spectacular display directly above me.

Sometimes good things take us away from something better. That happened to Martha, whose story is recorded in Luke 10:38–42. When Jesus and His disciples arrived in the village of Bethany, Martha welcomed them into her home. Being a good host meant that someone had to prepare the meal for the guests, so we don't want to be too hard on her.

When Martha complained to Jesus that her sister Mary wasn't helping, Jesus defended Mary's choice to sit at His feet. But the Lord wasn't saying that Mary was more spiritual than her sister. On occasion Martha seems to have shown more trust in Jesus than Mary did (John 11:19–20). And He wasn't being critical of Martha's desire to look after their physical needs. Rather, what the Lord wanted Martha to hear is that even in the busyness of our service, listening to Him is the main event.

Jesus Moment

How do you sit at Jesus's feet today? How do you make spending time with Him a top priority when life is so busy?

_____

_____

_____

_____

_____

_____

Lyrics for the Heart

I come to the garden alone,
While the dew is still on the roses;
And the voice I hear, falling on my ear,
The Son of God discloses.

And He walks with me, and He talks with me,
And He tells me I am His own,
And the joy we share as we tarry there,
None other has ever known.

"In the Garden," C. Austin Miles (1858–1946)

Jesus longs for our fellowship.

46

Surrounded by Prayer

The Context: Romans 15:22–33

I urge you, brothers and sisters, by our Lord Jesus Christ . . . ,
to join me in my struggle by praying to God for me. —Paul, Romans 15:30

My friend Melissa's nine-year-old daughter Sydnie was in the hospital for chemotherapy and a bone marrow transplant when I had a dream about her. I dreamed she was staying in a central room at the hospital with her parents. Surrounding her room was a block of other rooms where family and friends were staying and continually praying for her during her times of treatment.

In real life, Sydnie wasn't physically surrounded by family and friends in adjacent rooms. But spiritually speaking, she was surrounded by prayer and love throughout her life-and-death battle, which by God's grace, she won. God healed her.

The apostle Paul seemed to have a desire to be surrounded by prayer. In most of his letters to churches, he requested to be remembered in prayer to the Lord (2 Corinthians 1:11; Ephesians 6:18–20; Colossians 4:2–4; Philemon 22). To the believers in Rome, he wrote, "I urge you, brothers and sisters, . . . join me in my struggle by praying to God for me" (Romans 15:30). He knew that he could not be effective in his service for God without His power.

The Bible tells us that Jesus also prays for us (John 17:20; Hebrews 7:25), as does the Holy Spirit, whose prayers are according to the will of God (Romans 8:27). What a comfort to be surrounded by prayer!

Jesus Moment

What does it mean to you that Jesus himself prays for you? Think about Jesus turning to the Father in heaven and mentioning your name.

_____

_____

_____

_____

_____

_____

Key Words from the Word

"You help us by your prayers."
—*Paul to the people of Corinth, 2 Corinthians 1:11*

"Pray in the Spirit on all occasions with all kinds of prayers and requests. With this in mind, be alert and always keep on praying for all the Lord's people. Pray also for me."
—*Paul to the people of Ephesus, Ephesians 6:18–19*

"Devote yourselves to prayer, being watchful and thankful. And pray for us, too, that God may open a door for our message."
—*Paul to the people at Colossae, Colossians 4:2–3*

> Prayer is the autograph of God
> on the redeemed heart.

47

A Debtor

The Context: 2 Corinthians 5:12–17

Christ's love compels us. —Paul, 2 Corinthians 5:14

As a young man, Robert Robinson (1735–1790) enjoyed getting into trouble with his friends, so the stories go. At age seventeen, though, he heard a sermon by George Whitefield from Matthew 3:7, and he realized his need for salvation in Christ. The Lord changed Robinson's life, and he became a preacher. He also wrote several hymns, including his best-known "Come, Thou Fount of Every Blessing."

Lately I've been pondering God's amazing grace toward us and the last stanza of that hymn: "O to grace how great a debtor daily I'm constrained to be!" The hymn brings to mind the apostle Paul's words: "Christ's love compels [or constrains] us, because we are convinced that one died for all, and therefore all died. And he died for all, that those who live should no longer live for themselves but for him who died for them and was raised again" (2 Corinthians 5:14–15).

We can't earn God's love and grace. But because He has lavished it on us, how can we help but love Him in return by living for Him! I'm still learning what that looks like, but I think it includes drawing near to Him, listening to His Word, serving Him, and obeying Him out of gratitude.

As debtors, we owe it to Jesus to live each day for the One who gave himself for us.

Those who know God's grace show God's grace.

Jesus Moment

What is the difference between living for ourselves and living for Jesus? Does that change how we interact with others, how we treat our families, and how we spend our money? In what ways?

_____

_____

_____

_____

Action Steps

Sometimes we don't know exactly what it looks like to show adequate love for our Lord after all He has done for us. What might you need to focus on today?

- Drawing near to Him. Are there times during the day when you can pause and speak with the Lord, asking Him to surround you with His presence? To draw near?
- Listening to His Word. The Bible is a big, complicated book. What steps can you take to know where to start (or continue) reading it and learning what it is teaching you?
- Serving Him. We don't do things for God to win His favor or salvation, but we do honor Him when we put others first and find ways to help them in Jesus's name.
- Obeying Him out of gratitude and love. Our steps of obedience to God are acts of worship for Him, acts that say, "You are worthy of our good deeds."

_____

_____

48

Sweet Company

The Context: John 14:15–26

The Spirit of truth . . . lives with you and will be in you.
—*Jesus, John 14:17*

The elderly woman in the nursing home didn't speak to anyone or request anything. It seemed she merely existed, rocking in her creaky old chair. She didn't have many visitors, so one young nurse would often go into her room on her breaks. Without asking the woman questions to try to get her to talk, she simply pulled up another chair and rocked with her. After several months, the elderly woman said to her, "Thank you for rocking with me." She was grateful for the companionship.

Before He went back to heaven, Jesus promised to send a constant companion to His disciples. He told them He would not leave them alone but would send the Holy Spirit to be in them (John 14:17). That promise is still true for believers in Jesus today. Jesus said that the triune God makes His "home" in us (v. 23).

The Lord is our close and faithful companion throughout our entire life. He will guide us in our deepest struggles, forgive our sin, hear each silent prayer, and shoulder the burdens we cannot bear.

We can enjoy His sweet company today.

Jesus Moment

Imagine sitting alone with Jesus. When you read His words, or any of the Bible for that matter, and then pray to the Lord in earnest conversation, that is indeed what is happening. Get alone with Him, and then tell Him, "Thanks for sitting with me."

_____

_____

_____

_____

Key Words from the Word

"Don't you know that you yourselves are God's temple and that God's Spirit dwells in your midst?" —*Paul, 1 Corinthians 3:16*

"God's love has been poured out into our hearts through the Holy Spirit, who has been given to us." —*Paul, Romans 5:5*

"God sent the Spirit of his Son into our hearts, the Spirit who calls out, 'Abba, Father.'" —*Paul, Galatians 4:6*

The Christian's heart is the Holy Spirit's home.

49

Look What Jesus Has Done

The Context: Luke 8:1–8

See that you . . . excel in this grace of giving.
—Paul, 2 Corinthians 8:7

The little boy was only eight when he announced to his parents' friend Wally, "I love Jesus and want to serve Him in another country someday." Wally prayed for the boy as he watched him grow up. When this young man later applied with a mission agency to go to Mali, Wally told him, "It's about time! When I heard what you wanted to do, I invested some money and have been saving it for you, waiting for this exciting news." Wally has a heart for others and for getting God's good news to people.

Jesus and His disciples needed financial support as they traveled from one town and village to another, bringing the good news of His kingdom (Luke 8:1–3). A group of women who had been cured of evil spirits and diseases helped to support them "out of their own means" (v. 3). One was Mary Magdalene, who had been freed from the presence of seven demons. Another was Joanna, the wife of an official in Herod's court. Nothing is known about Susanna and "many others" (v. 3), but we know that Jesus had met their spiritual needs. Now they were helping Him and His disciples through giving financial resources.

When we consider what Jesus has done for us, His heart for others becomes our own. Let's ask God how He wants to use us.

> Jesus gave His all; He deserves our all.

Jesus Moment

God can use our time, our talents, our money, and our personalities for His good. Do an inventory to see what you have that can be used to point others to the love of Jesus. Get your kids involved too. Then make a plan to put it into action.

_____

_____

_____

_____

_____

_____

Action Steps

There are numerous ways to demonstrate a heart for others. Perhaps some of the following suggestions will be helpful as you serve others.

- Is there anyone in your church who may have been missing for a few weeks or who has been struggling with health or personal problems? You could write them a note as a representative of Jesus to someone who may be hurting.
- Are there any local organizations—perhaps that help young people—that your church supports: Bible clubs, youth outreach, Awana? How can you set aside time to show Jesus's love to the kids in one of those programs?
- *Another idea for serving others:* _____

_____

50

"Color Courage"

The Context: 1 Corinthians 4:10–17

Follow my example, as I follow the example of Christ.
—*Paul, 1 Corinthians 11:1*

A radio ad for watches suggests that listeners buy a watch with a bright color band and then wear it with clothes of other colors. When people notice your watch because of its contrasting color, the ad says, "They'll see that you have 'color courage.' And they'll want to be like you." Something in us enjoys having others follow our example.

If you do a quick reading of 1 Corinthians 4, you might think the apostle Paul sounds a bit boastful when he says to follow his example of self-sacrifice (v. 16). But a closer look at Paul's words shows why he wrote so confidently. He could ask people to imitate him because he imitated Christ (11:1), the greatest Servant of all.

The persecution he endured and the position he held in the church (4:10–17) all happened because Paul followed Jesus. When he mentioned that even if the Corinthians had ten thousand teachers he would still be their father in the faith (v. 15), he was acknowledging that Jesus is the only reason people could trust his teaching.

If we want people to imitate us, we must first imitate our Lord. If we have any reason for people to follow our example—if we have any courage to point others to the Savior—it is because of Him, not us.

> Others should imitate us only
> as far as we imitate Christ.

Jesus Moment

This is a great concept for parents, because they so much want their kids to imitate good characteristics and behaviors. So, in what areas should you begin to imitate Jesus as a guide for how you want the children you interact with (as teachers, aunts or uncles, parents, or grandparents) to act?

_____

_____

_____

_____

_____

_____

Thinking about Being Imitated

Think of the various roles you have in life and the many places where you engage with other people.

- As a parent relating to your child's teachers, administrators, and classmates.
- In the community as part of organizations.
- At church as you interact with fellow worshippers, whether they are old friends or people who walk in the door for the first time.

What can you do that imitates Jesus in front of others in these or other scenarios?

_____

_____

51

Heaven Rejoices

The Context: Luke 15:1–10

*There is rejoicing in the presence of the angels of God
over one sinner who repents. —Jesus, Luke 15:10*

Joann had been raised in a Christian home. But when she went to college, she began to question her beliefs, and she walked away from God. After graduation, she traveled to a number of countries, always looking for happiness but never feeling satisfied. When she experienced some difficulties, she recognized that God was pursuing her and that she needed Him.

From Germany, Joann called her parents in the United States and said, "I have given my life to Christ, and He's changing me! I'm sorry for the worry I've caused you." Her parents were so excited that they called her brothers and sisters-in-law to come over immediately. They wanted to tell them the exciting news in person. "Your sister has received Christ!" they said, rejoicing through tears.

The woman in Luke 15 who found her lost coin called her friends and neighbors together to rejoice with her (v. 9). Jesus told this story, and others about a lost sheep and a lost son, to the religious people of His day to show how He came to earth to pursue lost sinners. When we accept God's gift of salvation, there is rejoicing both on earth and in heaven. Jesus said, "There is rejoicing in the presence of the angels of God over one sinner who repents" (v. 10). How wonderful that Jesus has reached down to us and heaven rejoices when we respond!

Jesus Moment

Think about the last time you were able to rejoice with someone who trusted Jesus for the first time. What about that celebration is different from any other kind?

_____

_____

_____

_____

_____

Key Words from the Word

"I tell you that in the same way there will be more rejoicing in heaven over one sinner who repents than over ninety-nine righteous persons who do not need to repent." *—Jesus, Luke 15:7*

"Then I looked and heard the voice of many angels, numbering thousands upon thousands, and ten thousand times ten thousand. . . . In a loud voice they were saying: 'Worthy is the Lamb.'" *—John, Revelation 5:11–12*

"Praise him, all his angels; praise him, all his heavenly hosts." *—Psalmist, Psalm 148:2*

Angels rejoice when we repent.

52

Through the Cross

The Context: 2 Corinthians 4:8–18

[Nothing] will be able to separate us from the love of God
that is in Christ Jesus our Lord. —*Paul, Romans 8:39*

My former coworker Tom keeps an 8" by 12" glass cross on his desk. His friend Phil, who like Tom is a cancer survivor, gave it to him to help him look at everything "through the cross." The glass cross is a constant reminder of God's love and good purposes for him.

That's a challenging idea for all believers in Jesus, especially during difficult times. It's much easier to focus on our problems than on God's love.

The apostle Paul's life was certainly an example of having a cross-shaped perspective. He described himself in times of suffering as being "persecuted, but not abandoned; struck down, but not destroyed" (2 Corinthians 4:9). He believed that in the hard times, God is at work, "achieving for us an eternal glory that far outweighs them all. So we fix our eyes not on what is seen, but on what is unseen" (vv. 17–18).

To "fix our eyes . . . on what is unseen" doesn't mean we minimize the problems. Paul Barnett, in his commentary on this passage, explains, "There is to be confidence, based on the certainty of God's purposes for [us]. . . . On the other hand, there is the sober recognition that we groan with hope mingled with pain."

Jesus gave His life for us. His love is deep and sacrificial. As we look at life "through the cross," we see His love and faithfulness. And our trust in Him grows.

Jesus Moment

To imagine, at least in a small part, Jesus's love for you, think of times you did something sacrificial for someone you love. That great feeling of giving yourself up for another is a tiny picture of Jesus's amazing love for you.

_____

_____

_____

_____

_____

Lyrics for the Heart

Alas, and did my Savior bleed,
And did my Sovereign die?
Would He devote that sacred head
For sinners such as I?

At the cross, at the cross
Where I first saw the light,
And the burden of my heart rolled away,
It was there by faith I received my sight,
And now I am happy all the day!

"At the Cross," Isaac Watts (1674–1748)

Look at everything through the cross.

The Only King

The Context: Matthew 2:1–12

[The Magi] bowed down and worshiped [Jesus].
—*Matthew, Matthew 2:11*

As five-year-old Eldon listened to the pastor talk about Jesus leaving heaven and coming to earth, he gasped when the pastor thanked Him in prayer for dying for our sins. "Oh, no! He died?" the boy said in surprise.

From the start of Christ's life on earth, there were people who wanted Him dead. Wise men came to Jerusalem during the reign of King Herod inquiring, "Where is the one who has been born king of the Jews? We saw his star when it rose and have come to worship him" (Matthew 2:2). When the king heard this, he became fearful of one day losing his position to Jesus. So he sent soldiers to kill all the boys two years old and younger around Bethlehem. But God protected His Son and sent an angel to warn His parents to leave the area. They fled, and He was saved (vv. 13–18).

When Jesus completed His ministry, He was crucified for the sins of the world. The sign placed above His cross, though meant in mockery, read, "THIS IS JESUS, THE KING OF THE JEWS" (Matthew 27:37). Yet three days later He rose in victory from the grave. After ascending to heaven, He sat down on the throne as King of kings and Lord of lords (Philippians 2:8–11).

The King died for our sins—yours, mine, and Eldon's. Let's allow Him to rule in our hearts.

Jesus Moment

Jesus is the world's first and only truly benevolent king. What does it mean to let Him rule and reign in your life—especially knowing that He loves you and wants the best for you for His glory?

_____

_____

_____

_____

_____

_____

Communicating with Jesus

Dear Lord, thank you so very much for being willing to suffer such an excruciating and humiliating death on my behalf. You are the Creator, yet you allowed your creation to mistreat you and murder you as my substitute and to pay for my sins. You are indeed the Ruler of this universe, and I want to ask you to be the ruler of my life. Please help me to understand what it means to be subject to your benevolent rule and reign.

> Looking for a leader? Look to Jesus.

54

A Façade

The Context: Matthew 6:1–6

Give your gifts in private, and your Father, who sees everything, will reward you. —Jesus, Matthew 6:4 NLT

Kerri tries hard to get people to admire her. She acts happy most of the time so others will notice and compliment her on her joyful attitude. Some affirm her because they see her helping people in the community. But in a transparent moment Kerri will admit, "I love the Lord, but in some ways I feel like my life is a façade." Her own sense of insecurity is behind much of her effort of trying to look good to others, and she says she's running out of energy to keep it up.

We can probably all relate in some way, because it's not possible to have perfect motives. We love the Lord and others, but our motives for how we live the Christian life are sometimes mixed with our desire to be valued or praised.

Jesus talked about those who give, pray, and fast in order to be seen (Matthew 6:1–18). He taught in the Sermon on the Mount to "give your gifts in private," to "pray to your Father in private," and "when you fast, don't make it obvious" (vv. 4, 6, 16 NLT).

Serving is most often done publicly, but maybe a little anonymous service could help us learn to rest in God's opinion of us. He who created us in His image values us so much that He gave us His Son and shows us His love each day. Some things are best kept between Him and us.

Jesus Moment

How can it help your relationship with Jesus if you often dedicate yourself to alone time with Him? Service in public is needed, but private moments with the Lord are essential as well.

_____

_____

_____

_____

_____

Key Words from the Word

"Carry each other's burdens, and in this way you will fulfill the law of Christ." —Paul, *Galatians 6:2*

"Each of you should use whatever gift you have received to serve others, as faithful stewards of God's grace in its various forms." —Peter, *1 Peter 4:10*

"If anyone has material possessions and sees a brother or sister in need but has no pity on them, how can the love of God be in that person?" —John, *1 John 3:17*

Our desire to please God should be our highest motive for obeying God.

55

Our Covering

Blessed is the one whose transgressions are forgiven,
whose sins are covered. —*David, Psalm 32:1*

When talking about faith in Jesus, we sometimes use words without understanding or explaining them. One of those words is *righteous*. We say that God has righteousness and that He makes people righteous, but this can be a tough concept to grasp.

The way the word *righteousness* is pictured in the Chinese language is helpful. It is a combination of two characters. The top word is *lamb*. The bottom word is *me*. The lamb covers or is above the person.

When Jesus came to this world, John the Baptist called Him "the Lamb of God, who takes away the sin of the world" (John 1:29). We need our sin taken care of because it separates us from God, whose character and ways are always perfect and right. Because His love for us is great, God made His Son Jesus "who had no sin to be sin for us, so that in him we might become the righteousness of God" (2 Corinthians 5:21). Jesus, the Lamb, sacrificed himself and shed His blood. He became our "cover." He makes us righteous, which places us in right relationship with God.

Being right with God is a gift from Him. Jesus, the Lamb, is God's way to cover us.

Jesus Moment

It might be valuable to spend a little time studying the word *righteous* to see how the term relates to you and your relationship with Jesus. Can you truly be righteous? What does that look like?

_____

_____

_____

_____

_____

_____

Thinking about Righteousness

- We are all born unrighteous: "There is no one righteous, not even one" (Romans 3:10).
- Righteousness is not earned; it's a gift: "Righteousness is given through faith in Jesus Christ" (Romans 3:22).
- Righteous living leads to joy: "You have loved righteousness and hated wickedness; therefore God, your God, has set you above your companions by anointing you with the oil of joy" (Hebrews 1:9).

> The only permanent covering
> for sin is the blood of Christ.

56

Where to Find Hope

The Context: Romans 5:1–11

And hope does not put us to shame, because God's love has been poured out into our hearts through the Holy Spirit, who has been given to us.

—Paul, Romans 5:5

Elizabeth struggled for a long time with drug addiction, and when she recovered she wanted to help others in return. So she started writing notes and anonymously placing them throughout her city. Elizabeth tucks these notes under car windshield wipers and tacks them on poles in parks. She used to look for signs of hope; now she leaves them for others to find. One of her notes concluded with these words: "Much love. Hope sent."

Hope with love—that's what Jesus gives. He brings us His love with each new day and strengthens us with that hope. His love is not rationed out to us drop by drop but flows out of His heart freely and is poured lavishly into ours: "We know how dearly God loves us, because he has given us the Holy Spirit to fill our hearts with his love" (Romans 5:5 NLT). He desires to use the hard times to develop perseverance and character and bring us a satisfying, hope-filled life (vv. 3–4). And even when we're far from Him, He still loves us (vv. 6–8).

Are you looking for signs of hope? The Lord gives hope with love through inviting us to grow in a relationship with Him. Our hope for a fulfilling life is anchored in His unfailing love.

Jesus Moment

Do you have a hope-filled life, or do you sometimes feel hopeless? How can it help to realize that you have "the Holy Spirit to fill [your] heart with his love"? Knowing that, what steps can you take to gain hope?

_____

_____

_____

_____

_____

_____

Lyrics for the Heart

My hope is built on nothing less
Than Jesus' blood and righteousness;
I dare not trust the sweetest frame,
But wholly lean on Jesus' name.

On Christ, the solid rock, I stand;
All other ground is sinking sand.
All other ground is sinking sand.

"My Hope Is Built," by Edward Mote (1797–1874)

Hope is the anchor of the soul.

57

Can We Relax?

The Context: John 14:25–31

Do not let your hearts be troubled and do not be afraid.
—Jesus, John 14:27

Darnell entered the physical therapist's office knowing he would experience a lot of pain. The therapist stretched and bent his arm and held it in positions it hadn't been in for months since his injury. After holding each uncomfortable position for a few seconds, she gently told him: "Okay, you can relax." He said later, "I think I heard that at least fifty times in each therapy session: 'Okay, you can relax.'"

Darnell realized they could apply to the rest of his life as well. He could relax in God's goodness and faithfulness instead of worrying.

As Jesus neared His death, He knew His disciples would need to learn this. They'd soon face a time of upheaval and persecution. To encourage them, Jesus said He would send the Holy Spirit to live with them and remind them of what He had taught (John 14:26). So He could say, "Peace I leave with you; my peace I give you. . . . Do not let your hearts be troubled and do not be afraid" (v. 27).

There's plenty we could be uptight about in our everyday lives. But we can grow in our trust in God by reminding ourselves that His Spirit lives in us—and He offers us His peace. As we draw on His strength, we can hear Him in the therapist's words: "Okay, you can relax."

Teach me, Lord, to trust your faithfulness,
to know your presence, to experience your peace—to relax.

Jesus Moment

Did you need this today? Is there something that is bringing tension into your life? Can you hear Jesus saying to you, "Do not let your heart be troubled"? Ask Him to come alongside you; you'll discover that you can relax.

_____

_____

_____

_____

_____

Action Steps

Think through what is burdening your heart, and see if you can find some relief.

- What three things are most pressing on your heart right now? In what way can the Holy Spirit provide a calming presence in regard to those situations?

_____

_____

- What did Jesus do when things seemed to be pressing around Him? (Read Matthew 14:23 and Luke 6:12.) You may not have a mountain retreat, but you can still "get away" for a few moments to talk with God. What can you do today, and what can you plan to do later this year?

_____

_____

58

"Don't Forget Me"

The Context: Acts 1:1–11

He was taken up before their very eyes,
and a cloud hid him from their sight. —Luke, Acts 1:9

My niece, her four-year-old daughter Kailyn, and I had a wonderful Saturday afternoon together. We enjoyed blowing bubbles outside, coloring in a princess coloring book, and eating peanut butter and jelly sandwiches. When they got in the car to leave, Kailyn sweetly called out the opened window, "Don't forget me, Auntie Anne." I quickly walked toward the car and whispered, "I could never forget you. I promise I will see you soon."

In Acts 1, the disciples watched as Jesus was "taken up before their very eyes" into the sky (v. 9). I wonder if they thought they might be forgotten by their Master. But He'd just promised to send His Spirit to live in them and empower them to handle the persecution that was to come (v. 8). And He had taught them He was going away to prepare a place for them and would come back and take them to be with Him (John 14:3). Yet they must have wondered how long they would have to wait. Perhaps they wanted to say, "Don't forget us, Jesus!"

For those of us who have put our faith in Jesus, He lives in us through the Holy Spirit. We still may wonder when He will come again and restore us and His creation fully. But it will happen—He won't forget us. "Therefore encourage one another and build each other up" (1 Thessalonians 5:11).

Jesus Moment

Think about those words in 1 Thessalonians 5. The idea that Jesus would someday return was meant to encourage the believers. Things might be tough now, but Jesus will never abandon you. Your hope remains in Him and the reality of His future plans for you.

_____

_____

_____

_____

_____

Lyrics for the Heart

O the King is surely coming,
And the time is drawing nigh
When the blessed day of promise
We shall see;
Then the changing "in a moment,
In the twinkling of an eye,"
And forever in His
Presence we shall be.

"What a Gathering," Fanny Crosby (1820–1915)

We enjoy walking with you now,
but we look forward to the day when all things
will be fully restored. Come soon, Lord Jesus.

59

What Kind of Savior Is He?

The Context: John 6:47–51, 60–66

From this time many of his disciples turned back
and no longer followed him. —John, John 6:66

Some friends and I prayed for healing for three women battling cancer. We knew God had the power to do this, and every day we asked Him to do so. We had seen Him work in the past and believed He could do it again. There were days in each one's battle when healing looked like it was a reality, and we rejoiced.

But they all died during the fall of the year in which we had prayed for them. Some said that was "the ultimate healing," and in a way it was. Still the loss hurt us deeply. We wanted Him to heal them all—here and now. But for reasons we couldn't understand, no miracle came.

In New Testament times, some people followed Jesus for the miracles He performed and to get their needs met (John 6:2, 26). Others simply saw Him as the carpenter's son (Matthew 13:55–58), and another group expected Him to be their political leader (Luke 19:37–38). Some thought of Him as a great teacher (Matthew 7:28–29), while others quit following Him because His teaching was hard to understand (John 6:66).

Jesus still doesn't always meet our expectations of Him. Yet He is so much more than we can imagine. He's the provider of eternal life (vv. 47–48). He is good and wise; and He loves, forgives, stays close, and brings us comfort. May we find rest in Jesus and keep following Him.

Jesus Moment

Have you ever been among those who were tempted to stop following Jesus? Imagine what it means to turn from the Light of the World. The alternative is darkness and chaos. Stay in the Light. Stick with Jesus.

_____

_____

_____

_____

_____

_____

Key Words from the Word

"All authority in heaven and on earth has been given to me."
—*Jesus, Matthew 28:18*

"I am the way and the truth and the life. No one comes to the Father except through me." —*Jesus, John 14:6*

"Jesus Christ is the same yesterday and today and forever."
—*author, Hebrews 13:8*

"For in Christ all the fullness of the Deity lives in bodily form."
—*Paul, Colossians 2:9*

Jesus alone gives us the rest we need.

60

Run to the Cross

The Context: Hebrews 10:28–39

It is a dreadful thing to fall into the hands of the living God.
—author, Hebrews 10:31

Whenever a tsunami warning is given on the northern coastline of Maui, Hawaii, the people living in the community of Hana rush up the side of a mountain to a high place of safety. Nearby is a tall wooden cross that was placed there many years ago. For their physical safety from a possible flood, people run to the area where the cross is located.

In a similar way, all of us need a place of spiritual safety. Why? Because the Lord gives us these warnings in His Word: "All have sinned and fall short of the glory of God" and "the wages of sin is death" (Romans 3:23; 6:23). Hebrews 9:27 states: "It is appointed for men to die once, but after this the judgment" (NKJV). We might not like to think about what the consequences of our sin will be as we face a holy God, but it's a serious thing "to fall into the hands of the living God" (10:31).

The good news is that out of love for us, the Father has provided a place of safety! He sent His Son Jesus to die so we wouldn't have to be separated from Him forever (Romans 5:8–10; Colossians 1:19–22).

Because of Jesus Christ's death on the cross and His resurrection from the dead, that place of safety is available. Have you run to the cross?

Jesus Moment

What was your "run to the cross" moment? Think back to the time when you trusted Jesus as your Savior and recall how great that felt.

_____

_____

_____

_____

_____

Thinking about Safety

- Where do you feel most safe? Most likely it is in your home with the doors locked and surrounded by your family.

_____

_____

- Spiritually, what makes you feel safe? Does that have to be a place—such as church? Or can it be a place in your heart?

_____

_____

- Are you one hundred percent sure that you are safe in Jesus?

_____

_____

- Think of what it means to have the confidence of this verse: "You are my hiding place; you will protect me from trouble and surround me with songs of deliverance" (Psalm 32:7).

_____

_____

To escape sin's curse, run to the cross.

61

The Choice

The Context: Deuteronomy 30:15–20

I set before you today life and prosperity, death and destruction.

—Moses, Deuteronomy 30:15

You've heard the infamous name of John Wilkes Booth. He assassinated President Abraham Lincoln on April 14, 1865. But have you heard about Edwin Booth, John's eldest brother? Edwin, a well-known Shakespearean actor, was waiting at a Jersey City train station when he saw someone slip and fall off the platform. Edwin quickly grabbed the man's collar and pulled him to safety—rescuing him from serious injury or death. Who was the man he saved? Abraham Lincoln's son Robert, then a student at Harvard traveling home to Washington.

How ironic that the man who saved Lincoln's son had a brother who would soon kill the president! One saved a life; one took a life. One chose life; the other chose death.

The Lord gave His people—the Israelites who were soon to enter the Promised Land—a choice between life and death: They could love Him and obey His commands (Deuteronomy 30:16), or they could worship and serve other gods (v. 17). He told them, "I have set before you life and death, blessings and curses. Now choose life" (v. 19).

We too have a choice between life and death. We can receive Jesus as our Savior and live with Him forever, or we can reject Jesus and be in darkness forever without Him. The best choice is clear. Receive God's gift of His Son Jesus. Choose life!

Jesus Moment

This is the ultimate Jesus Moment—when you place your trust in Jesus Christ to forgive your sins, take you into God's family, and assure you of eternal life in His presence. Have you truly done this? When?

_____

_____

_____

_____

_____

Lyrics for the Heart

Just as I am, poor, wretched, blind;
Sight, riches, healing of the mind;
Yes, all I need, in Thee to find,
O Lamb of God, I come! I come!

Just as I am, Thou wilt receive,
Wilt welcome, pardon, cleanse, relieve;
Because Thy promise I believe,
O Lamb of God, I come! I come!

"Just As I Am," Charlotte Elliott (1789–1871)

The choice you make today will determine your tomorrow.

62

It's Up to God

The Context: Matthew 6:5–15

Your will be done. —Jesus, Matthew 6:10

Nate and Sherilyn enjoyed their stop at an *omakase* restaurant while visiting New York City. *Omakase* is a Japanese word that translates, "I will leave it up to you," which means customers at such restaurants let the chef choose their meal. Even though it was their first time to try this type of cuisine and it sounded risky, they loved the food the chef chose and prepared for them.

That idea could carry over to our attitude toward God with our prayer requests: "I will leave it up to you." The disciples saw that Jesus "often withdrew to lonely places" to pray (Luke 5:16), so they asked Him one day to teach them how to pray. He told them to ask for their daily needs, forgiveness, and the way out of temptation. Part of His response also suggested an attitude of surrender: "Your will be done, on earth as it is in heaven" (Matthew 6:10).

We can pour out our needs to the Lord because He wants to hear what's on our hearts—and He delights to give. But being human and finite, we don't always know what's best, so it only makes sense to ask with a humble spirit, in submission to Him. We can leave the answer to Him, confident that He's trustworthy and will choose to prepare what's good for us.

Thank you, God, for carrying me and my needs close to your heart. I surrender my life and those I love to your care.

Jesus Moment

If you were to give God your needs and give Him a list of options to choose, you might miss the best He has for you. This is why we need to say "your will be done." How can this be applied to upcoming decisions?

_____

_____

_____

_____

_____

Thinking about God's Will

Some aspects of God's will are discernable to us, meaning we have to deduce what God's will is for us. What is the criteria for discerning God's will in these areas, according to Romans 12:2? What might be examples of God's discernable will for us?

_____

_____

Some aspects of God's will are spelled out for us. Look at these passages and see what we are all required to do under the will of the Lord:

- 1 Thessalonians 5:18 _____
- 1 Peter 2:15 _____
- 1 Thessalonians 4:3 _____
- Ephesians 5:17 _____

63

Beautiful Fruit; Beautiful Life

The Context: Luke 8:4–8, 11–15

The seed is the word of God.

—Jesus, Luke 8:11

"Kids should be able to throw a seed anywhere they want [in the garden] and see what pops up," suggests Rebecca Lemos-Otero, founder of City Blossoms. While this is not a model for careful gardening, it reflects the reality that each seed has the potential to burst forth with life. City Blossoms has created gardens for schools and neighborhoods in low-income areas. The kids are learning about nutrition and gaining job skills through gardening. Rebecca says, "Having a lively green space in an urban area . . . creates a way for kids to be outside doing something productive and beautiful."

Jesus told a story about the scattering of seed that had the potential of producing "a hundred times more than was sown" (Luke 8:8). That seed was God's good news planted on "good soil," which He explained is "honest, good-hearted people who hear God's word, cling to it, and patiently produce a huge harvest" (v. 15 NLT).

The only way we can be fruitful, Jesus said, is to stay connected to Him (John 15:4). As we're taught by Christ and cling to Him, the Spirit produces in us His fruit of "love, joy, peace, forbearance, kindness, goodness, faithfulness, gentleness and self-control" (Galatians 5:22–23). He uses the fruit He produces in us to touch the lives of others, who are then changed and grow fruit from their own lives. This makes for a beautiful life.

Jesus Moment

As you abide in Jesus, the true vine, you have the ability not only to grow stronger but also to bear fruit. As you scatter the seed of the Word of God, you can watch with joy as a harvest appears.

Thinking about the Fruit of the Spirit

For each of the fruit of the Spirit as spelled out in Galatians 5, think of a way you could display that trait to someone in the next few days:

- Love: _____

  _____

- Joy: _____

  _____

- Peace: _____

  _____

- Forbearance: _____

  _____

- Kindness: _____

  _____

- Goodness: _____

  _____

- Faithfulness: _____

  _____

- Gentleness: _____

  _____

- Self-control: _____

  _____

Our hope is anchored in Jesus.

64

Jordan's Idea

The Context: 2 Timothy 3:14–17

All Scripture is God-breathed and is useful for teaching, rebuking, correcting and training in righteousness. —Paul, 2 Timothy 3:16

One spring day, Jordan began asking questions about Jesus's resurrection as his mom was taking him to preschool. When she realized that he thought Jesus was rising from the dead for the first time that Easter, she tried to correct him. She pulled the car over and told him all about Jesus's death and resurrection. She concluded, "Jesus rose from the dead a long time ago, and now He wants to live in our hearts." But Jordan still didn't understand.

Unsure how she could make it any clearer, she said, "How about if we stop by the bookstore? I saw some books about Easter when I was there last week. We'll get one and read through it together." With wisdom beyond his years, Jordan responded, "Can't we just read the Bible?"

Jordan's idea was right. Commentaries and books about the Bible are helpful tools. But they aren't a substitute for God's revelation of himself—His Word.

No other book is "God-breathed" (2 Timothy 3:16). As author Eugene Peterson said, "God's voice [is] speaking to us, inviting, promising, blessing, confronting, commanding, healing."

When we want to know more about Jesus, let's follow Jordan's idea and go first to the ultimate source of truth about Him—the Bible.

Jesus Moment

It might be valuable to read again the story of Jesus's death, burial, and resurrection—in God's own words—in the Bible (Matthew 27:11–28:10). What do you learn from that?

_____

_____

_____

_____

_____

Inspiring Words

"I have a fundamental belief in the Bible as the Word of God, written by those who were inspired. I study the Bible daily."
—Isaac Newton, British scientist (1643–1727)

"I believe the Bible is the best gift God has ever given to man. All the good from the Savior of the world is communicated to us through this Book." —Abraham Lincoln, American president (1809–1865)

"To what greater inspiration and counsel can we turn than to the imperishable truth to be found in this Treasure House, the Bible?"
—Elizabeth II, Queen of England

Go to the Bible for your protection, correction, and direction.

65

A Place of Belonging

The Context: Ephesians 3:14–21

So that Christ may dwell in your hearts through faith.
—*Paul, Ephesians 3:17*

Some years after the tragic loss of their first spouses, Robbie and Sabrina fell in love, married, and combined their two families. They built a new home and named it Havilah (a Hebrew word meaning "writhing in pain" and "to bring forth"). It signifies the making of something beautiful through pain. The couple says they didn't build the home to forget their past but "to bring life from the ashes, to celebrate hope." For them, "it is a place of belonging, a place to celebrate life and where we all cling to the promise of a future."

That's a beautiful picture of our life in Jesus. He pulls our lives from the ashes and becomes for us a place of belonging. When we receive Him, He makes His home in our hearts (Ephesians 3:17). God adopts us into His family through Jesus so we belong to Him (1:5–6). Although we'll go through painful times, He can use even those to bring good purposes in our lives.

Daily we have opportunity to grow in our understanding of God as we enjoy His love and celebrate what He's given us. In Him, there's a fullness to life that we couldn't have without Him (3:19). And we have the promise that this relationship will last forever. Jesus is our place of belonging, our reason to celebrate life, and our hope now and forever.

Jesus Moment

What does it mean to belong to Jesus? In quiet moments of meditation and prayer, do you feel His presence and His care? Do you sense Him dwelling in your heart?

_____

_____

_____

_____

_____

_____

Inspiring Words

"Not only do we not know God except through Jesus Christ; we do not even know ourselves except through Jesus Christ."
—*Blaise Pascal, French theologian (1623–1662)*

"You don't realize that Jesus is all you need until Jesus is all you have." —*Timothy Keller, American pastor*

"God doesn't just give us grace; He gives us Jesus, the Lord of grace." —*Joni Eareckson Tada, American author, speaker*

> The name of Jesus is the heart of our faith
> and the foundation of our hope.

66

What's Your Motto?

The Context: Luke 12:4–7, 22–32

Don't be afraid; you are worth more than many sparrows.

—*Jesus, Luke 12:7*

Grug Crood, the dad of a caveman family in an animated movie, believes that there's no safe place beyond their cave. The family huddles together at night so he can protect them. He thinks his teenage daughter should give up her adventurous side because it can only lead to danger. His motto for his family is "Never not be afraid." In other words, "Always be afraid."

Jesus often told His followers the opposite: "Don't be afraid." He said that to Simon when He called him to follow Him (Luke 5:10). When Jairus, a synagogue leader whose daughter was dying, came to Him, Jesus reassured him with those same words of care (8:50).

Luke 12 records Jesus telling His disciples not to be afraid when He taught them how God cared for them much more than for the sparrows (v. 7). And after His resurrection, Jesus told the women who came to the tomb, "Do not be afraid" (Matthew 28:9–10).

Fear is a universal feeling. We have concerns about loved ones, our needs, and the unknown future. How can we learn to have faith? The Lord has given us a foundation on which to build our confidence in Him: "God has said, 'Never will I leave you; never will I forsake you.' So we say with confidence: 'The Lord is my helper; I will not be afraid'" (Hebrews 13:5–6).

Jesus Moment

What do you fear most? Possible loss of a loved one? Poor health? Financial failure? Lack of friends? Can you hear Jesus say to Jairus, "Don't be afraid"? Can you hear Him saying it to you? Can you then say, "The Lord is my helper; I will not be afraid"?

_____

_____

_____

_____

_____

Lyrics for the Heart

Why should I feel discouraged?
Why should the shadows come?
Why should my heart be lonely
And long for heaven and home?
When Jesus is my portion,
My constant friend is He:
His eye is on the sparrow
And I know He watches me.

"His Eye Is on the Sparrow," Civilla D. Martin (1866–1948)

The love of God frees us from the prison of fear.

67

A Missing Sheep

The Context: Luke 15:1–10

We are his people, the sheep of his pasture.
—*psalmist, Psalm 100:3*

Laura loaded a borrowed goat and sheep into a trailer to transport them to church for a rehearsal of a live nativity. The animals head-butted and chased each other for a bit and then settled down. Laura started for the church but first had to stop for gas.

While pumping the gas, she noticed the goat standing in the parking lot! And the sheep was gone! In the commotion of getting them settled, she had forgotten to lock one of the latches. Laura called the sheriff and some friends who searched frantically during the last daylight hours. Many were praying that she would find the borrowed animal.

The next morning Laura and a friend went out to post "Lost Sheep" flyers. At one local business, a customer overheard them asking the cashier about posting a flyer and said, "I think I know where your sheep is!" The sheep had wandered to his neighbor's farm, where he had put it in the barn for the night.

That search reminds us of God's love for His lost sheep—including you and me. Jesus came from heaven to earth to show us His love and provide salvation (John 3:16). He goes to great lengths to seek and find us (Luke 19:10). When the sheep was found, Laura nicknamed her Miracle. Sounds about right for Christians as well, for our salvation is a miracle of God's grace.

"The good shepherd gives His life for the sheep." *John 10:11 (NKJV)*

Jesus Moment

Have you ever thought about the miracle of salvation? What are some miracles that had to happen for Jesus's sacrifice to take place—including the miracle that you heard the message of the gospel?

_____

_____

_____

_____

_____

Thinking about the Miracle of Salvation

Is there anyone you know—whether a friend or a relative—about whom you would say, "It would be a miracle for that person to come to Christ"? Can you think of any New Testament characters whose salvation was miraculous?

_____

_____

How do you go about searching for people who need to know about Jesus? Do you make a list? Do you pray about them? Is there anything you can do to make them realize they need a Savior?

_____

_____

68

Your Death

The Context: Romans 6:1–14

*Do not let sin reign in your mortal body
so that you obey its evil desires. —Paul, Romans 6:12*

Cathy and 8,500 other patients of a local hospital received their bills, along with some shocking news: They had died!

Cathy said, "I was pretty sure I was not dead, but you never know." Turns out, it was just a computer glitch—just "a pretty funny story to tell and a small annoyance."

You may be surprised to learn about your own "death" when you read Romans 6:6, "Our old self was crucified with [Christ], . . . that we should no longer be slaves to sin." If you are a follower of Jesus, you "died to sin" (v. 2).

But we still sin, so what does it mean to be "crucified with Him"? It means we no longer have to be overpowered by temptation. We can choose to obey God through His power.

We can now "live a new life" (v. 4) in which sin does not control us. One day, when we are resurrected to live with the Lord Jesus, we'll be completely removed from the presence of sin forever.

Our greatest freedom is freedom from sin.

Jesus Moment

What serves as your greatest incentive to choose to obey the Lord?
What do Jesus's life and words teach us about avoiding temptation?

_____

_____

_____

_____

_____

Inspiring Words

"Believers will not experience perfect deliverance from sin in this
age, so that they never sin at all. What has been shattered is not
the presence of sin but the mastery of sin over believers."
—*Thomas Schreiner, American Bible scholar*

"The gospel is this: We are more sinful and flawed in ourselves
than we ever dared believe, yet at the very same time we are more
loved and accepted in Jesus Christ than we ever dared hope."
—*Timothy Keller, American pastor*

"I couldn't live in peace if I put the shadow of a willful sin
between myself and God."
—*Mary Ann Evans (Pen name: George Eliot), British author (1819–1880)*

69

Struggling with Addiction

The Context: Hebrews 4:14–16

God is faithful. —Paul, 1 Corinthians 10:13

Eric was struggling with an addiction, and he knew it. His friends and family members encouraged him to stop. He agreed that it would be best for his health and relationships, but he felt helpless. When others told him how they had quit their bad habits, he replied, "I'm happy for you, but I can't seem to stop! I wish I had never been tempted in the first place. I want God to take the desire away right now."

Immediate deliverance may happen for some, but most face a daily battle. While we don't always understand why the temptation doesn't go away, we can turn to God on whatever path we find ourselves. And perhaps that is the most important part of our struggle. We learn to exchange our futile efforts to change for complete dependence on God.

Jesus was tempted also, just as we are, so He understands what we're feeling (Mark 1:13). He sympathizes with our struggles (Hebrews 4:15), and we can "come boldly to the throne of grace, that we may obtain mercy and find grace to help in time of need" (v. 16 NKJV). He also uses others, including trained professionals, to lean on along the way.

Whatever battles we may be facing today, we know this—God loves us much more than we can imagine, and He is faithful to come to our assistance.

Jesus Moment

Which do you believe is stronger: an addiction you may have or the power of Jesus to release you from that hook? The phrase "God is faithful," and the Hebrews writer's promise that we "find grace to help in time of need" are words to cling to in your battles.

_____

_____

_____

_____

_____

Action Steps

- The first step in tackling a difficult problem is naming it. What is a difficulty that is holding you back spiritually?

_____

_____

- Sometimes it is helpful to have a safe friend—a trusted Christian friend—with whom you can discuss the issue. Who might be that person for this difficulty?

_____

_____

- If you can find scriptural help for what you are facing, you can have additional confidence. What Scriptures relate to this issue?

_____

_____

- If this problem involves sin, how can 1 John 1:9 help you?

_____

_____

We are not tempted because we are evil;
we are tempted because we are human.

70

An Ordinary Guy

The Context: John 10:31–42

Though John never performed a sign, all that John said about [Jesus] was true. —many people, John 10:41

Steve was just an ordinary guy. He quietly served in a church I attended years ago. He helped prepare communion, shoveled the church sidewalks in the winter, and mowed the lawn in the summer. He spent time with teenage boys who had no fathers in the home. I often heard him telling people at church in his quiet way how good the Lord was to him. During prayer meeting he didn't talk much about himself; instead, he would ask us to pray for the people he was introducing to Jesus.

A verse in John 10 about John the Baptist makes me think of Steve. People said of him: "Though John never performed a sign, all that John said about [Jesus] was true" (v. 41). John didn't perform miracles as Jesus did. He didn't talk about himself but came "as a witness to testify concerning that light, so that through him all might believe" (1:7). He said of Jesus, "Look, the Lamb of God, who takes away the sin of the world!" (1:29). My friend Steve bore witness of "that light" as well.

Our aim, as followers of Jesus, is to do the same—to "testify concerning that light." We're just ordinary people, serving God in our little corner of the world. With our quiet deeds and words, let's point others to the Light!

Jesus Moment

As you think of things such as your social media presence, your conversations with your friends, and your interactions with people you are just getting to know, how much of that ordinary conversation includes mentions of Jesus and His importance? What challenge does that question pose?

_____

_____

_____

_____

_____

Communicating with Jesus

Dear Lord, you know how ordinary I am. Sometimes being "just a normal person" holds me back from telling others about you. Who am I to tell others what to do? So, help me, Lord, to know that you are the subject of those attempts, not me. Help me to stop focusing on my ordinary self and talk about my extraordinary Savior!

Christians are ordinary people who are committed to the extraordinary person of Christ.

71

It's Beautiful

The Context: Mark 14:3–9

Leave her alone. . . . Why are you bothering her?
She has done a beautiful thing to me. —Jesus, Mark 14:6

After being away on business, Terry wanted to pick up some small gifts for his children. The clerk at the airport gift shop recommended a number of costly items. "I don't have that much money with me," he said. "I need something less expensive." The clerk tried to make him feel that he was being cheap. But Terry knew his children would be happy with whatever he gave them, because it came from a heart of love. And he was right—they loved the less-expensive gifts he bought.

During Jesus's last visit to the town of Bethany, Mary wanted to show her love for Him (Mark 14:3–9). So she brought "an alabaster jar of very expensive perfume, made of pure nard" and anointed Him (v. 3). The disciples asked angrily, "Why this waste?" (Matthew 26:8). Jesus told them to stop troubling her, for "she has done a beautiful thing to me" (Mark 14:6). He delighted in Mary's gift to Him, for it came from a heart of love. Even anointing Him for burial was beautiful!

What would you like to give to Jesus to show your love? Your time, talent, treasure? It doesn't matter if it's costly or inexpensive, whether others understand it or criticize it. Whatever is given to our Savior from a heart of love is beautiful to Him.

Jesus Moment

If Jesus were to appear to you and you had one thing to offer Him out of love and devotion, what would it be? Why is He worthy of this gift from you even though you can't see Him?

_____

_____

_____

_____

_____

Lyrics for the Heart

Jesus paid it all,
All to Him I owe;
Sin has left a crimson stain,
He washed it white as snow.

And when before the throne
I stand in Him complete,
"Jesus died my soul to save,"
My lips shall still repeat.

"Jesus Paid It All," Elvina Hall (1820–1889)

A healthy heart beats with love for Jesus.

72

Truly Amazing

The Context: Romans 5:6–11

*See what great love the Father has lavished on us,
that we should be called children of God! —John, 1 John 3:1*

I read these words on a young woman's personal website: "I just want to be loved—and he has to be amazing!"

Isn't that what we all want—to be loved, to feel cared for by someone? And so much the better if he or she is amazing!

The one who fits that description most fully is Jesus Christ. In a display of unprecedented, unselfish love, He left His Father in heaven and came to earth as the baby we celebrate at Christmas (Luke 2). Then, after living a perfect life, He gave His life as an offering to God on the cross in our behalf (John 19:17–30). He took our place because we needed to be rescued from our sin and its death penalty. "While we were still sinners, Christ died for us" (Romans 5:8). Then three days later, the Father raised Jesus to life again (Matthew 28:1–8).

When we repent and receive Jesus's gift of amazing love, He becomes our Savior (John 3:16–18), Lord (John 13:14), Teacher (Matthew 23:8), and Friend (John 15:14). "See what great love the Father has lavished on us, that we should be called children of God!" (1 John 3:1).

Looking for someone to love you? Jesus loves us so much more than anyone else possibly could. And He is truly amazing!

Jesus Moment

Think of someone who loves you with a deep, warm, caring love. Jesus loves you that much and more. No matter what you are going through or how down you get about troubling circumstances, Jesus's amazing love is always there to lift you up and encourage you.

_____

_____

_____

_____

Lyrics for the Heart

All hail the power of Jesus' name!
Let angels prostrate fall.
Bring forth the royal diadem,
And crown Him Lord of all!

Oh, that with all the sacred throng
We at his feet may fall!
We'll join the everlasting song
And crown Him Lord of all.

"All Hail the Power," Edward Perronet (1721–1792)

The wonder of it all—just to think that Jesus loves me.

73

No Smiling Policy

The Context: John 13:31–35

By this everyone will know that you are my disciples,
if you love one another. —*Jesus, John 13:35*

Usually we're told to smile before someone takes our picture. But in some parts of the US, a no-smiling policy is enforced when getting a photo taken for a driver's license. Because of identity theft, these motor vehicle departments carefully check new photos that are taken to be sure they don't match photos already in the system. If someone gets a picture taken under a false name, an alarm is sent to the operator.

From 1999 to 2009, one state stopped six thousand people from getting fraudulent licenses. But why no smiling? The technology recognizes a face more easily if the person has a neutral facial expression.

Jesus prescribed a good way to recognize a Christian—and it most probably includes a smile. Jesus told His disciples, "By this everyone will know that you are my disciples, if you love one another" (John 13:35). The ways to show love to fellow believers are as endless as there are people with needs: a note of encouragement, a visit, a meal, a gentle rebuke, a prayer, a Bible verse, a listening ear, even just a friendly smile.

The apostle John wrote, "We know that we have passed from death to life, because we love each other" (1 John 3:14). Can others recognize, by our care for fellow Christians, that we know and love the Lord?

Jesus Moment

Will others recognize Christ in any of these common scenarios? Going through the checkout line at the grocery store. Coaching or cheering for a child's sporting event. Being served by the wait staff at a restaurant (including the tip). Interacting with a salesperson while buying shoes or clothes.

_____

_____

_____

_____

_____

Inspiring Words

"We must show our Christian colors if we are to be true to Jesus Christ." —C. S. Lewis, British author (1898–1963)

"You can always give without loving, but you can never love without giving." —Amy Carmichael, British missionary (1867–1951)

"What does love look like? It has the hands to help others. It has the feet to hasten to the poor and needy. It has eyes to see misery and want. It has ears to hear the sighs and sorrows of men. That is what love looks like." —Augustine, Roman theologian (354–430)

> One measure of our love for God is how much we show love to His children.

74

Free Pizza!

The Context: John 6:25–41

I am the bread that came down from heaven.
—Jesus, John 6:41

Money is tight when you're a college student. So when free food is available, students will show up anytime, anywhere. If a company wants to recruit new employees, it will entice young people on college campuses to come to a presentation by offering free pizza. Some students attend presentation after presentation—just for the pizza. The food in the present seems to be more important than the job for the future.

Jesus fed a crowd of five thousand hungry people, and the next day many went looking for Him (John 6:10–11, 24–25). He challenged them: "You are looking for me, not because you saw the signs I performed but because you ate the loaves and had your fill" (v. 26). It seems that the food was more important to some of the people than the everlasting life Jesus offered in himself. He told them He was "the bread of God . . . that comes down from heaven and gives life to the world" (v. 33). Some didn't believe, wouldn't accept His teaching, and "no longer followed him" (v. 66). They wanted the food, but they didn't want Him and what would be required of them to follow Him.

Jesus calls us today to come to Him—not for the blessings from His hand but to receive the eternal life He offers and to follow Him, "the bread of God."

Jesus Moment

Sometimes it is a challenge to move from "what's in it for me?" regarding your faith to "what is required of me?" to serve Jesus. Although your salvation is free, what are some things Jesus wants you to do in obedience to Him?

_____

_____

_____

_____

_____

_____

Key Words from the Word

"Submit yourselves, then, to God. Resist the devil, and he will flee from you. Come near to God and he will come near to you."
—James, James 4:7–8

"Carry each other's burdens, and in this way you will fulfill the law of Christ." —Paul, Galatians 6:2

"Whatever you do, work at it with all your heart, as working for the Lord." —Paul, Colossians 3:23

> Only Christ, the Living Bread,
> can satisfy our spiritual hunger.

75

An Easy Yoke

The Context: Matthew 11:25–30

*Take my yoke upon you and learn from me, for I am gentle
and humble in heart, and you will find rest for your souls.
For my yoke is easy and my burden is light. —Jesus, Matthew 11:29–30*

A Sunday school teacher read Matthew 11:30 to the children in her class, and then asked: "Jesus said, 'My yoke is easy.' What is a yoke?" A boy replied, "A yoke is something they put on the necks of animals so they can help each other."

The teacher asked, "What is the yoke Jesus puts on us?" A quiet little girl whispered, "It is God putting His arm around us."

When Jesus came, He offered an "easy" and "light" yoke compared to the yoke of the religious leaders (Matthew 11:30). They had placed "heavy, cumbersome loads" of laws on the people (Matthew 23:4; Acts 15:10), which no one could possibly keep.

God knew we would never be able to measure up to His standards (Romans 3:23), so He sent Jesus to this earth. Jesus bore the punishment of death for our sins. As we recognize our need for forgiveness, Jesus comes alongside us. He places His yoke on us, freeing us from guilt and giving us His power to live in a God-pleasing way.

Do you need Jesus's help? He says, "Come to me. . . . Take my yoke upon you and learn from me" (Matthew 11:28–29). He longs to put His arm around you.

Jesus Moment

In what ways do you sense Jesus coming alongside you to help in burdensome moments? He promises to do so, but what attitude do you need if you want to sense His presence?

_____

_____

_____

_____

Inspiring Words

"The command of Jesus is hard, unutterably hard, for those who try to resist it. But for those who willingly submit, the yoke is easy, and the burden is light."
—*Dietrich Bonhoeffer, German pastor (1906–1945)*

"We must quit bending the Word to suit our situation. It is we who must be bent to that Word, our necks that must bow under the yoke." —*Elisabeth Elliot, American missionary, author (1926–2015)*

"When one is yoked to Jesus Christ, that which is performed is the joy of the true disciple."
—*J. Dwight Pentecost, American Bible scholar (1915–2014)*

> God's easy yoke does not fit on a stiff neck.

76

Bring Them to Jesus

The Context: Luke 18:15–17

*Let the little children come to me, and do not hinder them,
for the kingdom of God belongs to such as these. —Jesus, Luke 18:16*

The Scripture reading from Luke 18 about children seemed unusual at the memorial service for David Holquist. After all, he was seventy-seven when he died.

Yet the pastor said the verses fit David, a longtime college professor, perfectly. Part of his legacy was that he took time for children—his own and others'. He made balloon animals and puppets, and he helped in a puppet ministry at church. When planning worship services with others, he frequently asked, "What about the children?" He was concerned about what would help the children—not just the adults—to worship God.

Luke 18 shows us the concern Jesus had for children. When people brought little ones to Him, the disciples wanted to protect Jesus, a busy man, from the bothersome children. But it seems that Jesus was not at all bothered by them. Just the opposite. He said, "Let the little children come to me, and do not hinder them" (v. 16). Mark adds that Jesus took them in His arms and blessed them (10:16).

Let's examine our own attitude about children and then follow the example of men and women like David Holquist. Find ways to help the children come to Jesus.

Jesus Moment

Children are the coolest humans on earth. They are loving and caring and eager to learn. Find ways to help your children and the children of others to learn about Jesus and His love for them. Like Jesus, say, "Let the little children come to me."

_____

_____

_____

_____

Key Words from the Word

"Behold, children are a heritage from the LORD, the fruit of the womb a reward." —*Solomon, Psalm 127:3 (ESV)*

"See that you do not despise one of these little ones. For I tell you that their angels in heaven always see the face of my Father in heaven." —*Jesus, Matthew 18:10*

"A woman giving birth to a child has pain because her time has come; but when her baby is born she forgets the anguish because of her joy that a child is born into the world." —*Jesus, John 16:21*

God has great concern for little children.

77

Where Do I Start?

The Context: Luke 11:1–10

*I call on the L*ORD *in my distress, and he answers me.*

—*psalmist, Psalm 120:1*

Several years ago, I was driving on the freeway when my car died. I pulled over to the side of the road, got out of the car, and opened the hood. As I looked at the engine, I thought, *A lot of good this does me. I know nothing about cars. I don't even know what I'm looking for! Where do I start?*

That's how we might sometimes feel about prayer: Where do I start? That's what the disciples wanted to know when they said to Jesus, "Teach us to pray" (Luke 11:1). The best place to look for instruction is in the example and teaching of Jesus. Perhaps you can begin with these two questions:

Where should we pray? Jesus prayed in the temple, in the wilderness (Luke 4), in quiet places (Matthew 14:22–23), in the garden of Gethsemane (Luke 22), and on the cross (Luke 23:34, 46). He prayed alone and with others. Look at His life, follow His example, and pray wherever you are.

What should we pray? In the Lord's Prayer (Luke 11), Jesus taught us to ask that God's name be honored and that His will be done on earth as it is in heaven. Ask Him for your daily provisions, for forgiveness of sin, and for deliverance from temptation and evil (Luke 11:2–4).

So if you're looking for a good place to start, follow the example of the Lord's Prayer.

If Jesus needed to pray, how can we do less?

Jesus Moment

Some people recite the Lord's Prayer daily. Others use it as a template for their own prayers. Either way, asking the Father how to live in a way that brings Him honor, requesting His will to be done, relying on Him for our provisions, pleading for forgiveness, and seeking help for temptation make up a pretty good prayer.

_____

_____

_____

_____

_____

_____

Action Steps

Think through your prayer patterns. These ideas might be helpful in starting fresh in talking to God.

- Some people find it helpful to have a "set-aside" place to pray. Maybe just a chair with a side table with a Bible, a notebook, and a devotional book.
- Another getting-started tip is to see if there is a specific time during the day to designate for prayer. Make an appointment with God.
- Use the elements of the Lord's Prayer as a guide: honor God; God's will; daily provisions; freedom from sin; praise.
- *My plan:* _____

_____

78

Prayer Circles

The Context: Luke 18:9–14

All those who exalt themselves will be humbled.

—Jesus, Luke 18:14

Around the circle the sixth grade girls went, taking turns praying for each other in the Bible study group. "Father in heaven," Anna prayed, "please help Tonya not to be so boy-crazy." Tonya added with a giggle, "And help Anna to stop acting so horrible in school and bothering other kids." Then Talia prayed, "Lord, help Tonya to listen to her mother instead of always talking back."

Although the requests were real, the girls seemed to enjoy teasing their friends by pointing out their flaws in front of the others instead of caring about their need for God's help. Their group leader reminded them about the seriousness of talking to almighty God and the importance of evaluating their own hearts.

If we use prayer to point out the faults of others while ignoring our own, we're like the Pharisee in Jesus's parable. He prayed, "God, I thank you that I am not like other people—robbers, evildoers, adulterers—or even like this tax collector" (Luke 18:11). Instead, we're to be like the man who asked God to be merciful to him, "a sinner" (v. 13).

Our prayers shouldn't become a listing of others' flaws. The kind of prayer God desires flows out of a humble evaluation of our own hearts.

Jesus Moment

Even if you do pray in private for those you know are struggling with sin, your attitude needs to be one of total humility—aware of your own frailty. And perhaps you begin with asking God's forgiveness for your sins.

_____

_____

_____

_____

_____

Communicating with Jesus

I come to you today, Lord, asking you to help me focus my prayers on what is essential to growth in Christlikeness. Each time I talk with you, help me to concentrate on your greatness. When I make a request, Lord, help it to be about what is important to you. Allow my intercessory prayer for others to center on what they need from you. Help my prayer life, Lord, to be divinely focused, not controlled by human interests.

The highest form of prayer comes from the depths of a humble heart.

79

The Little Evangelist

The Context: Mark 12:28–34

*Love the Lord your God with all your heart and with all your soul
and with all your mind and with all your strength. —Jesus, Mark 12:30*

My six-year-old neighbor Michael and I were talking in my front yard
when two new neighbor kids stopped by. After I asked them their names,
Michael's first question to them was: "Do you love God?" Sugar, a five-
year-old boy, quickly responded, "No!" Michael gave him a look of disap-
proval and concern. When four-year-old Nana noticed he wasn't pleased
with that answer, she said, "Yes!"

Michael's "witnessing strategy" may not be the most effective, but he
does have an important question for the people he meets (and I've heard
him ask it of several others as well).

Jesus was asked, "Of all the commandments, which is the most important?" (Mark 12:28). He answered, "'The Lord is one. Love the Lord your
God with all your heart and with all your soul and with all your mind and
with all your strength'" (vv. 29–30).

Jesus was referring to Old Testament times—during which God had
told the Israelites to place Him as the one and only God in their lives and
nation. The pagan nations around them had many gods they loved and
worshipped, but God's people were to be different.

Jesus said loving God is to be our top priority too. So, Michael wants to
know, "Do you love God?"

Jesus Moment

Spend a few moments thinking of the implications of the two great commandments: Love God; love others. Which of the two could use a little more attention in your life?

_____

_____

_____

_____

Key Words from the Word

"Love the Lord your God with all your heart and with all your soul and with all your strength and with all your mind."
—a teacher of the Law, Luke 10:27

"What does the LORD your God ask of you but to fear the LORD your God, to walk in obedience to him, to love him, to serve the LORD your God with all your heart and with all your soul?"
—Moses, Deuteronomy 10:12

"Keep yourselves in God's love as you wait for the mercy of our Lord Jesus Christ to bring you to eternal life." —Jude, Jude 21

> If you truly love the Lord,
> you'll want others to love Him too.

80

Thunderstorm Thoughts

The Context: Matthew 8:23–27

The God of peace will be with you.

—Paul, Philippians 4:9

I laugh every time I hear the radio commercial that has a woman shouting to her friend in conversation. She's trying to talk above the sounds of the thunderstorm in her own head. Ever since a storm damaged part of her home, that's all she hears because her insurance company isn't taking care of her claims.

I've heard thunderstorms in my head, and maybe you have too. It happens when a tragedy occurs—to us, to someone close to us, or to someone we hear about in the news. Our minds become a tempest of "what-if" questions. We focus on all the possible bad outcomes. Our fear, worry, and trust in God fluctuate as we wait, pray, grieve, and wonder what the Lord will do.

It's natural for us to be fearful in a storm (literal or figurative). The disciples had Jesus right there in the boat with them, yet they were afraid (Matthew 8:23–27). He used the calming of the storm as a lesson to show them who He is—a powerful God who also cares for them.

We wish that Jesus would always calm the storms of our life as He calmed the storm for the disciples that day. But we can find moments of peace when we're anchored to the truth that He's in the boat with us and He cares.

Jesus Moment

What storms are thundering their way through your mind and heart? Would it help to put the words THE GOD OF PEACE WILL BE WITH YOU on an index card and tape it where you can see it throughout the day? And remember, Jesus is in the boat with you.

_____

_____

_____

_____

_____

Lyrics for the Heart

The Lord's our Rock, in Him we hide
A shelter in the time of storm;
Secure whatever ill betide
A shelter in the time of storm.

O Jesus is a Rock in a weary land,
A weary land, a weary land;
O Jesus is a Rock in a weary land
A shelter in the time of storm.

"A Shelter in the Time of Storm," Vernon J. Charlesworth (1838–1915)

To realize the worth of the anchor,
we need to feel the stress of the storm.

81

A Gift of Shelter

There was no guest room available for them.

—Luke, Luke 2:7

Life was tough for Datha and her family. At age thirty-nine, she had a heart attack, which led to bypass surgery. Then she learned that she had coronary artery disease. A year later, her fifteen-year-old daughter Heather became paralyzed as the result of a car accident. Datha quit her job to take care of Heather, and the bills started piling up. Soon they would be facing eviction. Datha was so angry with God that she stopped praying.

Then came Christmas Eve. A young girl knocked on Datha's door. The girl wished her a "Merry Christmas," gave her an envelope, and left quickly. Inside was a gift that would cover Datha's housing needs for the next year. The attached note read, "Please accept this gift in honor of the Man whose birthday we celebrate on this holy night. Long ago, His family also had a shelter problem."

Luke 2 tells the story of Joseph and Mary as they searched for a shelter for Mary to deliver her baby. They found a place with the animals. Later in His life, Jesus said of himself, "The Son of Man has no place to lay his head" (Matthew 8:20).

Jesus understood Datha's troubles. He brought her hope and met her needs through others who contributed funds.

We can cast all our cares on Him (1 Peter 5:7). In our God, we find shelter (Psalm 61:3–4).

Jesus Moment

There are two sides to Datha's story: Datha's needs and the young girl's generosity. We are all on one side of this or the other. Talk to Jesus about your situation: Does He want you to be a giver or a receiver? Trust Him either way.

_____

_____

_____

_____

_____

Action Steps

As you consider the visitor to Datha's door and how she changed Datha's life, what are some ways you can take similar action?

- Who have you heard about recently in your circle of influence who has a specific need you can help meet? In what way do you feel the Spirit leading you to help?
- There are many ways to help those who struggle. How can you encourage someone you know? A quick text to say you are thinking about her? A card in the mail to share some thoughts and words of hope? An email that just says, "I'm praying for you" (immediately followed by prayer)?
- *Another idea:* _____

    _____

One measure of our love for Christ
is our sensitivity to the needs of others.

82

Fever Pitch

The Context: Matthew 22:34–40

Love your neighbor as yourself. —*Jesus, Matthew 22:39*

In the movie *Fever Pitch*, Ben Wrightman is crazy about the Boston Red Sox baseball team. He rarely misses a game during the spring and summer months.

One winter, Ben falls in love with a young woman named Lindsey and wins her heart. Then spring rolls around, and she finds out that he's a different person during baseball season. He has no time for her unless she goes to the games with him.

When Lindsey ends her relationship with Ben because of his fanaticism, he talks with a young friend, who says, "You love the Sox. But tell me, have they ever loved you back?" Those words cause Ben to analyze his priorities and to give more time to the woman he loves, who loves him back.

We pour our lives into hobbies, pleasures, activities, work—many good things. But two things should always be thought about when making our choices. Jesus said, "Love the Lord your God with all your heart. . . . Love your neighbor as yourself" (Matthew 22:37, 39).

When it seems our life is getting out of balance, the question, "Has that hobby or activity or thing ever loved me back?" may help to keep us in check. Loving God and loving people are what really count.

Jesus Moment

So many good things vie for our attention. Are you feeling any imbalance currently in what occupies your time compared with what should? How can talking with Jesus about this make a difference?

_____

_____

_____

_____

_____

_____

Inspiring Words

"You cannot love a fellow creature fully till you love God."
—C. S. Lewis, British author (1898–1963)

"The world does not understand theology, but it understands love." —Dwight L. Moody, American evangelist (1837–1899)

"When we show love to others, God's presence is with us."
—Linda Evans Shepherd, American writer

> We show our love for God
> when we share His love with others.

83

Breath Mint, Anyone?

The Context: Galatians 6:1–5

Carry each other's burdens, and in this way
you will fulfill the law of Christ. —*Paul, Galatians 6:2*

I once heard of a website that helped people tell a coworker what they were afraid to say in person. Comments like: "A breath mint would be beneficial" or "Your cell phone ringer is very loud" or "Your perfume/cologne is very strong on a regular basis." Users of this service could confront issues anonymously by having an email message sent for them.

It's understandable that we're cautious in talking to others about something that bothers us. But when it comes to confronting fellow believers about their sin, that's serious. We might wish we could do it anonymously, yet we may have to do it face-to-face.

Galatians 6:1–5 offers some guidelines for confronting a fellow Christian who is living a sinful lifestyle. The first requirement is that we're close to the Lord ourselves, and that we don't exalt ourselves as superior to the one who is sinning. Then we are to look at the situation as restoring the person, not bringing condemnation. We're to have a spirit of gentleness, all the while keeping in mind that we too may be tempted. Jesus also gave instructions that can help us with issues of sin against us personally (Matthew 7:1–5; 18:15–20).

With God's enablement we can courageously and sensitively confront and restore others.

Jesus Moment

This is a touchy situation, and it has to be handled correctly if God is to be honored. There has to be self-reflection, prayer, and loving confrontation. Read Matthew 18:15–17 before taking such a step. The desire is always restoration.

_____

_____

_____

_____

_____

Key Words from the Word

"Brothers and sisters, if someone is caught in a sin, you who live by the Spirit should restore that person gently. But watch yourselves, or you also may be tempted." —*Paul, Galatians 6:1*

"As iron sharpens iron, so one person sharpens another." —*Solomon, Proverbs 27:17*

"Take special note of anyone who does not obey our instruction in this letter. Do not associate with them, in order that they may feel ashamed. Yet do not regard them as an enemy, but warn them as you would a fellow believer." —*Paul, 2 Thessalonians 3:14–15*

> To help people get back on the right path,
> walk with them and show them the way.

84

Retirement Time?

The Context: Matthew 16:24–28

Whoever loses their life for me will find it.
—*Jesus, Matthew 16:25*

After working for forty years as a teacher, Jane Hanson retired. She and her husband were looking forward to the arrival of their first grandchild.

Retirement is that time of life when many people simply relax, travel, or enjoy hobbies. But Jane heard about a ministry to at-risk youth in a city near her home, and she knew she had to get involved. "I realized there are kids just waiting, and I could make a difference," she said. She began teaching English to a young Liberian man who had been forced to flee his home country because of civil war. Though he was in a safe environment, he didn't understand the new language. Of this ministry opportunity, Jane said with a smile, "I could just go shopping to stay busy, but what fun would that be?"

Jane is making a difference. Perhaps she has learned a little of what Jesus meant when He said, "Whoever wants to save their life will lose it, but whoever loses their life for me will find it" (Matthew 16:25). Giving ourselves to the Lord through helping others takes self-denial, yet one day Jesus will reward that effort (v. 27).

Let's follow Jane's example of love for God and others—no matter what our stage of life may be.

Work for the Lord—His retirement plan is out of this world.

Jesus Moment

Perhaps you don't have the extra free time Jane had. How else can you help someone—by giving of your talents to those who need your help? You don't serve Jesus out of guilt, but out of your love for Him.

_____

_____

_____

_____

_____

Action Steps

Is it time to evaluate your current involvement in Christ-honoring ministries and pray over your future involvement? Maybe these suggestions could help.

- Does your church have any ministries that you could be involved with in your community? Bible clubs in schools or community service groups for children? Should you get involved in one of those?
- If you can no longer participate physically in a local group reaching out with the gospel, could you become a prayer partner for a ministry? Perhaps a crisis pregnancy center or missionary family your church supports?
- Sometimes we wait for people to ask us to support a God-centered ministry financially. Should you take the initiative to do some research and find out what important work needs monetary support and give it before being asked?

_____

_____

85

From Sunset to Sunrise

The Context: Hebrews 9:24–28

Just as people are destined to die once, . . . so Christ was sacrificed once to take away the sins of many. —author, *Hebrews 9:27–28*

Kariel was riding home from a children's program at church with her neighbor friends. Admiring the sunset, she said to Gini, the driver, "That sunset is so beautiful it looks like heaven!" So Gini asked her, "Do you know how to get to heaven?" Kariel, who was only six, answered confidently, "You have to have Jesus as your Savior—and I do!" Then she began to ask her friends in the van if they knew Jesus too.

That same evening, Kariel's thirteen-year-old sister Chantel was at another church, where someone asked her if she had a relationship with Jesus. She told the person she did.

Early the next morning, fire swept through Kariel and Chantel's home, and tragically, they both died. They were in heaven with Jesus at sunrise.

No one has the promise of tomorrow. The crucial question is this: Have we admitted our need for God's forgiveness of our sin and trusted Jesus as our Savior? (Romans 3:23; John 1:12). Our sin separates us from God and requires judgment, but Jesus gave His life in our place (Hebrews 9:27–28).

Make sure you have the same confidence that Chantel and Kariel had. Then, when your time comes to die, you'll be in heaven with Jesus at the next sunrise.

Jesus Moment

If you are confident of your salvation, do you know any Chantels or Kariels who need to know that Jesus loves them? Why not ask Jesus for an opportunity to tell a child about His love in the next few days?

_____

_____

_____

_____

_____

_____

Key Words from the Word

"Repent, for the kingdom of heaven has come near."
—John the Baptist, Matthew 3.2

"Seek the LORD while he may be found; call on him while he is near." —Isaiah, Isaiah 55:6

"You also must be ready, because the Son of Man will come at an hour when you do not expect him." —Jesus, Matthew 24:44

Sunset in one land is sunrise in another.

86

Reach Out to the Young

The Context: Mark 10:13–16

[Jesus] took the children in his arms, placed his hands
on them and blessed them. —Mark, Mark 10:16

Darmeisha didn't like the neighbor woman Suzanne, but she still knocked at her door frequently. Darmeisha was an unhappy eight-year-old who seemed to enjoy mocking people. Most of their conversations ended with Suzanne telling her that she needed to go home.

Suzanne didn't like Darmeisha, but she knew the little girl had reasons for her attitude—living in poverty, having no father in her life, and being neglected by her mother. So Suzanne asked the Lord to help her love Darmeisha. She began greeting her with a smile and showing an interest in her life. Darmeisha gradually warmed up to her and they became friends.

Years went by, and they began doing a Bible study together. They talked about what it meant to follow Jesus, because Darmeisha gave her life to Him.

Jesus took time for children. He was "indignant" when the disciples wanted to keep the little ones away from Him, and He said, "Let the little children come to me, and do not hinder them" (Mark 10:13–14). He even said that we all must receive His kingdom as children do (v. 15).

A Barna survey revealed that eighty-five percent of Christians began their relationship with Jesus before age fourteen. So take time for the children. Reach out to the young.

Jesus Moment

What are a few good ways to introduce children to Jesus? Are there some children in your sphere of influence whom you could guide toward a saving knowledge of the Savior?

_____

_____

_____

_____

_____

Thinking about Children

- Children need to be introduced to Jesus. At what age do you think children are old enough to understand their need for salvation? What are ways to introduce them to Him before they are truly old enough to understand sin and repentance?

_____

_____

- Children have questions. What are some ways to begin discussing spiritual things with children? And what do you do with answers that seem to be too difficult to explain to them? Does your church have resources to help you with this kind of thing?

_____

_____

- Children love to be read to. If there are children in your home or who visit your home, do you have a library of good books and specifically God-centered books to read to them? Do you seek to read to them regularly?

_____

_____

> Strong faith is often found in the heart of a child.

87

Three Needs

The Context: 1 John 4:7–21

We know and rely on the love God has for us. God is love.

—*John, 1 John 4:16*

I've heard it said that there are three things a person needs to be happy:

1. Something to do—meaningful work or helping others.
2. Someone to love—someone to whom we can give of ourselves, such as a spouse, a child, or a friend.
3. Something to look forward to—a vacation, a visit from a loved one, improved health, the realization of a dream.

Those things may bring some temporary happiness. But for lasting fulfillment, they can all be found in a relationship with Jesus, God's Son.

Something to do. As believers, we have been given gifts from the Holy Spirit to serve our Savior by serving others in God's family (Romans 12:1–16). We are also called to spread the gospel around the world (Matthew 28:19–20).

Someone to love. We love God because He first loved us (1 John 4:19). And we love others, "for love comes from God" (v. 7).

Something to look forward to. One day we'll be welcomed into God's presence forever, where we will enjoy a perfect place prepared especially for us (John 14:2–3; Revelation 21:3–4). We'll see Jesus and be like Him (1 John 3:2).

For lasting fulfillment, Jesus Christ truly is everything we need.

Jesus Moment

In which of the "somethings" above are you most lacking? Ask the Lord to give you just what you need for His glory: a valuable task or a person who needs your caring love or a goal to strive for.

_____

_____

_____

_____

_____

Action Steps

- "Doing" is usually not something we struggle with. There is plenty to do. But then we have to think about priorities. Try listing fifteen things you did today and then evaluate the value of each thing done. Keep in mind that sometimes, doing things for relaxation is not a bad thing!

_____   _____   _____

_____   _____   _____

_____   _____   _____

_____   _____   _____

- Some people are easier to love than others. But if we are to love others as we love ourselves, we can't really be choosy. Who is someone who is hard to love but needs your touch of kindness?

_____

- Looking forward to something great is fun: A vacation in the sun. A day off from work or school. A fun activity with the family. Do you look forward to heaven with a similar anticipation?

_____

_____

> Where there's hope, there's happiness.

88

Praying Sheep

The Context: James 1:1–8

You may ask me for anything in my name,
and I will do it. —*Jesus, John 14:14*

Two children who were dressed as sheep in the Christmas play at Kaw Prairie Community Church in De Soto, Missouri, had a special part. Whenever Murphy, the main character in the play, encountered a problem, the sheep (Maria and Luke) came onstage to offer a reminder of what he needed to do. One carried the sign: "Just." The other carried the sign: "Pray."

We've all been faced with situations when we didn't know what to do, or there was nothing we could do. When we're distressed, we probably don't want to hear someone flippantly say, "Just pray!" That answer seems too simplistic and can even feel hurtful if it's said unthinkingly.

But the simple suggestion "Just pray" is exactly what we need to do. During the days of the early church, James wrote to believers who were going through serious trials—difficulties that most of us know nothing about: stonings, imprisonment, and beatings for their faith. He told them to ask God for the wisdom and comfort to withstand those trials: "You should ask God, who gives generously to all without finding fault, and it will be given to you" (1:5).

When you encounter a problem, remember the simple instructions of the "Just Pray" sheep and talk to Jesus about it. He'll meet your needs His way.

Jesus Moment

Jesus is your Shepherd, and He knows your voice. A shepherd stops at nothing to keep His sheep where they should be. What do you as a praying sheep need from your Shepherd?

_____

_____

_____

_____

_____

Inspiring Words

"Prayer is the open admission that without Christ we can do nothing. Prayer humbles us as needy and exalts God as wealthy."
—John Piper, American pastor (1946–)

"Prayer opens the way for God himself to do His work in us and through us." —Andrew Murray, South African pastor (1828–1917)

"We have to pray with our eyes on God, not on the difficulties."
—Oswald Chambers, British Bible teacher (1874–1917)

"Prayer lays hold of God's plan and becomes the link between His will and its accomplishment on earth."
—Elisabeth Elliot, American missionary, author (1926–2015)

Those who wait on the Lord shall renew their strength.

89

A Learner

The Context: Luke 2:46–52; Isaiah 50:4–6

They found [Jesus] in the temple courts, sitting among the teachers,
listening to them and asking them questions. —*Luke, Luke 2:46*

The poster in the church hallway pictured a young boy dressed in Middle Eastern clothing, with Bible in hand, walking up a hill to church. The caption read: "Jesus was a good Christian boy who went to Sunday school every Sunday."

As a Jewish boy, Jesus didn't go to Sunday school and church on Sunday, so the poster was inappropriate. But the picture is correct in portraying Jesus's desire to be in His Father's temple to listen to His teaching.

When Jesus was twelve, He went with His parents to Jerusalem for the Feast of the Passover (Luke 2:41–42). On their way home, His parents realized He was not with them. When they returned, they "found him in the temple courts, sitting among the teachers, listening to them and asking them questions" (v. 46).

Jesus had the heart of a learner-disciple. Isaiah writes of Him as Jehovah's Servant: "The Sovereign Lord . . . wakens me morning by morning, wakens my ear to listen like one being instructed. The Sovereign Lord has opened my ears" (50:4–5). In His humanity, the Son was open to learn from His Father.

Jesus's example is strong. It challenges us to be listeners to God's Word. We too can become learner-disciples if we'll keep our hearts open to God's teaching.

Jesus Moment

It is amazing that Jesus was a learner. How much more should we, who know so little, strive to learn like the One who knew everything. What new efforts can you make to know God better?

_____

_____

_____

_____

Action Steps

Are you looking for ways to enhance your understanding of God's Word? Here are a few ideas that might help you set aside time to do that.

- Set realistic expectations: Learn a little each time.
- Find the right place: Discover a location that is conducive to quiet contemplation.
- Reserve a daily time: Are you a morning person? An evening person? Plan accordingly.
- Be consistent, even if time is short: Make it a calendar priority.
- *Another idea:* _____

_____

> The highest goal of learning is to know God.

90

Reminders of Love

The Context: John 19:1–7, 16–18

God is love. —John, 1 John 4:8

After the United States entered World War II in 1941, Estelle tried to talk her boyfriend, Sidney, out of joining the Army. But he enlisted and began his training in April of the following year. For the next three years he wrote her love letters—525 in all. Then in March 1945, she learned that her beloved fiancé had been killed in combat.

Although Estelle did eventually marry, the memories of her first love lived on in her heart. To honor that love, she published a book of Sidney's wartime correspondence more than sixty years later.

Like those letters, the Scriptures are a reminder of the Lord's love. He says: "I have loved you with an everlasting love; I have drawn you with unfailing kindness" (Jeremiah 31:3).

Jesus said, "As the Father has loved me, so have I loved you. Now remain in my love" (John 15:9). The Bible also tells us that "Christ loved the church and gave himself up for her" (Ephesians 5:25). "[Jesus] gave himself for us to redeem us" (Titus 2:14).

"God is love" (1 John 4:8).

Read the Scriptures often and be reminded that Jesus loves you and died for you.

Jesus Moment

It would seem appropriate to spend a few moments and thank God for His reminders of love—especially everything Jesus has done on your behalf.

_____

_____

_____

_____

_____

Key Words from the Word

"For God so loved the world that he gave his one and only Son, that whoever believes in him shall not perish but have eternal life." —*John, John 3:16*

"Greater love has no one than this: to lay down one's life for one's friends." —*Jesus, John 15:13*

"For Christ's love compels us, because we are convinced that one died for all, and therefore all died. And he died for all, that those who live should no longer live for themselves but for him who died for them and was raised again." —*Paul, 2 Corinthians 5:14–15*

> Nothing can compare to the love of God.

91

Nailed to the Cross

The Context: Colossians 2:9–17

God made you alive with Christ. He forgave us all our sins.
—Paul, Colossians 2:13

It was a touching church service. Our pastor talked about Jesus taking our sins upon himself and dying in our place to take our punishment. He asked if anyone still felt guilt over confessed sins and was therefore not enjoying the forgiveness of God.

We were to write the sin or sins on a piece of paper, walk to the front of the church, and nail the paper to the cross that was placed there. Many went forward, and you could hear the pounding of nails for several minutes. That act didn't give us forgiveness, of course, but it was a physical reminder that Jesus had already taken those sins on himself as He hung on the cross and died.

That's what the apostle Paul taught the church at Colossae. The people were being influenced by false teachers who presented Christ as less than adequate for their needs. But Paul explained how wrong that was. He reminded them that Jesus paid the price for our sins. He said, "The charge of our legal indebtedness, which stood against us and condemned us; he has taken it away, nailing it to the cross" (Colossians 2:14).

If we confess our sin to God, seeking His cleansing, He will forgive (1 John 1:9). We don't need to hold on to the guilt. Our sins have been nailed to the cross; they've been taken away. Jesus has forgiven them all.

Jesus Moment

Are any sins still trying to condemn you—stealing your joy and the rights of freedom that Jesus provided when He forgave you at the time of your salvation? Maybe you could do what the pastor recommended—write them down and then symbolically nail them to the cross.

_____

_____

_____

_____

_____

Lyrics for the Heart

Marvelous grace of our loving Lord,
Grace that exceeds our sin and our guilt,
Yonder on Calvary's mount outpoured,
There where the blood of the Lamb was spilt.

Grace, grace, God's grace,
Grace that will pardon and cleanse within;
Grace, grace, God's grace,
Grace that is greater than all our sin.

"Grace Greater Than Our Sin," Julia H. Johnston (1919–1949)

Guilt is a burden God never intended His children to bear.

92

Loved Well

The Context: Ephesians 3:14–21

I pray that you . . . may have power . . . to grasp how wide and long and high and deep is the love of Christ. —Paul, Ephesians 3:17–18

We were gathered with family for Thanksgiving dinner when someone asked if each person would share what he or she was thankful for. One by one we talked. Three-year-old Joshua was thankful for "music," and Nathan, aged four, for "horses." We were all silenced, though, when Stephen (who was soon to turn five) answered, "I'm thankful that Jesus loves me so well." In his simple faith, he understood and was grateful for the love of Jesus for him personally. He told us that Jesus showed His love by dying on a cross.

The apostle Paul wanted the believers in the church at Ephesus to understand how well God loved them, and that was his prayer: "That [they would] . . . have power, together with all the Lord's holy people, to grasp how wide and long and high and deep is the love of Christ" (Ephesians 3:17–18). He prayed that they would be rooted and grounded in that love.

To ground ourselves in God's love, it would be helpful to review these verses frequently or even memorize them. We can also take a few minutes each day to thank the Lord for the specific ways He shows His love to us. This will help us to grow in our belief and be thankful—as Stephen is— that Jesus loves us "so well."

Jesus Moment

Think of the ways Jesus loves you. Think of the blessings of forgiveness, the help of His guidance through the Holy Spirit, and the numerous other ways He directs your path.

_____

_____

_____

_____

_____

_____

Communicating with Jesus

Dear Lord, I realize that I don't thank you enough for all that you have given me. I could begin at creation—thanking you for the magnificent world you've created—and move all the way through your great story to find ways to thank you. For today, please accept my gratitude for your great love, which brought you here to earth to die for us. And thank you for the salvation that death and your resurrection provided for us. Thank you for the hope of eternal life you've provided.

To renew your love for Christ, review Christ's love for you.

93

The Arlington Ladies

The Context: Matthew 26:6–13

Wherever this gospel is preached throughout the world,
what she has done will also be told, in memory of her. —*Jesus, Matthew 26:13*

In 1948, the US Air Force Chief of Staff noticed that no one attended the funeral of one of his airmen at Arlington National Cemetery, and that deeply disturbed him. He talked with his wife about his concern that each soldier be honored at burial, and she began a group called the Arlington Ladies.

Someone from the group honors each deceased soldier by attending his or her funeral. The ladies also write personal notes of sympathy and speak words of gratitude to family members when they are present. If possible, a representative keeps in contact with the family for months afterward.

Margaret Mensch, an Arlington Lady, says, "The important thing is to be there for the families. . . . It's an honor to . . . pay tribute to the everyday heroes that make up the armed forces."

Jesus showed the importance of paying tribute. After a woman poured a costly, fragrant oil on His head, He said that she would be honored for, as it turned out, centuries to come (Matthew 26:13). The disciples were indignant and thought her act was wasteful, but Jesus called it "a good work" (v. 10 NKJV) for which she would be remembered "wherever this gospel is preached throughout the world" (v. 13).

We know heroes who have given their lives in service to their country. Let's honor them while we remember as well heroes of the faith through the centuries.

Jesus Moment

Who do you consider a hero of the faith? Can you tell his or her story to others as a way to expose new people to the gospel story?

_____

_____

_____

_____

_____

Key Words from the Word

"Honor your father and your mother." —*God, Deuteronomy 5:16*

"The elders who direct the affairs of the church well are worthy of double honor." —*Paul, 1 Timothy 5:17*

"Honor all people. Love the brotherhood. Fear God. Honor the king." —*Peter, 1 Peter 2:17 NKJV*

"You shall rise before the gray headed and honor the presence of an old man, and fear your God: I am the LORD."
—*God, Leviticus 19:32 NKJV*

> We honor God when we honor one another.

94

Imagine That!

The Context: 2 Peter 1:16–21

Do your best to present yourself to God as one approved, . . .
who correctly handles the word of truth. —Paul, 2 Timothy 2:15

My friends and I were anticipating a contemplative time looking at a collection of artwork about Jesus's parable of the prodigal son who returned home to a forgiving father (Luke 15). When we arrived at the information table, we noticed the brochures, books, and a sign pointing to the artwork.

Also on the table was a dinner plate with bread, a napkin, and a glass. Each of us privately pondered what the significance of the plate could be. We wondered if it represented communion fellowship between the prodigal son and his father when he returned home. But as we examined it more closely, a surprising and humorous reality struck us simultaneously: Someone had left a dirty plate on the display table. And it wasn't bread, but leftover cookie bars! Our imaginations had been wrong.

We had a good laugh, but then it made me think about how sometimes we imagine more than what's really there while reading the Bible. Rather than assuming that our speculation is always correct, however, we need to be sure our interpretation fits with the whole of Scripture. Peter said that "no prophecy of Scripture is of any private interpretation" (2 Peter 1:20 NKJV). As we depend on the Spirit's instruction, a careful study of the context, and the wisdom of respected Bible teachers, we'll avoid seeing things in the Word that aren't really there.

Jesus Moment

What are some ways to make sure you don't misinterpret Scripture and apply it incorrectly? Even some of Jesus's parables are a bit hard to understand. What are some good tools to use to get the right understanding?

_____

_____

_____

_____

_____

_____

Thinking about Bible Study

Before you begin digging into Scripture, keep a few guidelines in mind as you study:

- Have confidence in the Bible: The entire Book was given us through inspiration and is profitable (2 Timothy 3:16).
- Ask for the help of the Holy Spirit. Jesus told us in John 14:26 that the Holy Spirit would "teach you all things." Allow Him to guide your thinking.
- Submit to God's authority in Scripture.

> A text out of context is often a dangerous pretext.

95

The Good Story

The Context: Luke 23:44–24:3

They found the stone rolled away from the tomb, but when they entered, they did not find the body of the Lord Jesus. —Luke, Luke 24:2–3

People tend to remember negative images more than they do positive ones, according to an experiment conducted at the University of Chicago. While people say they want to turn away from the barrage of bad news in the media—tragedies, diseases, economic downturns—this study suggests that their minds are drawn to the stories.

Katherine Hankey (1834–1911) was more interested in the "good news." She had a great desire to see young women come to know Christ. In 1866, she became very ill. As she lay in bed, she thought about all those with whom she had shared the story of Jesus's redemption, and she wished that someone would visit and comfort her with "the old, old story." That's when she wrote the poem that later became a hymn, "Tell Me the Old, Old Story":

> Tell me the story slowly, that I may take it in—
> That wonderful redemption, God's remedy for sin.
> Tell me the story often, for I forget so soon.

We never tire of hearing the story of God's great love, which led Him to send His one and only Son to this earth (John 3:16). Jesus lived a perfect life, took our sin upon himself when He was crucified, and three days later rose again (Luke 23:44–24:3). When we receive Him as our Savior, we are given eternal life and become His children (John 1:12). That's really good news!

Jesus Moment

Who told you the good news about Jesus? Can you imagine life without a Savior? Is there anyone who needs to hear about Him from you?

_____

_____

_____

_____

_____

_____

Lyrics for the Heart

Tell me the story of Jesus,
Write on my heart every word.
Tell me the story most precious,
Sweetest that ever was heard.
Tell how the angels in chorus,
Sang as they welcomed His birth,
"Glory to God in the highest!
Peace and good tidings to earth."

"Tell Me the Story of Jesus," Fanny Crosby (1820–1915)

The good news of Christ is the best news in the world.

96

A Bouquet of Praise

The Context: 1 Peter 4:7–11

. . . that in all things God may be praised through Jesus Christ.
—Peter, 1 Peter 4:11

Corrie ten Boom (1892–1983) was a World War II concentration camp survivor and Christian who became a popular speaker around the world. Thousands attended her meetings as she talked about how she had learned to forgive her captors just as Christ had forgiven her sins.

After each meeting, people surrounded her and heaped accolades on her for her godly qualities and thanked her for encouraging them in their walk with the Lord. Corrie said she would then return to her hotel room, get down on her knees, and present those compliments in thanks to God. She called it giving God "a bouquet of praise."

The Lord has given each of us gifts to use to minister to one another (1 Peter 4:10) so that "in all things God may be praised through Jesus Christ. To him be the glory and the power for ever and ever" (v. 11). We have nothing to offer others that we have not first received from the Lord (1 Corinthians 4:7), so the glory does belong to Him.

To learn humility, perhaps we could follow Corrie's example. If we receive a compliment for something we've said or done, let's privately give a bouquet of praise to God for the glory He alone deserves.

Jesus Moment

People such as Corrie ten Boom have set wonderful examples for us to follow. If you haven't read it, pick up her book *The Hiding Place* to get a picture of what she went through during the time of the Holocaust in the 1940s. What Christians from history have been an inspiration to you?

_____

_____

_____

_____

Inspiring Words

"Doth not all nature around me praise God? If I were silent,
I should be an exception to the universe."
—*Charles Spurgeon, British preacher (1834–1892)*

"Whatever troubles are weighing you down are not chains.
They are featherweight when compared to the glory yet to come."
—*Joni Eareckson Tada, American author (1949–)*

"We would worry less if we praised more. Giving thanks is the enemy of discontent and dissatisfaction."
—*Harry Ironside, Canadian-American preacher (1876–1951)*

Praise is the fairest blossom that springs from the soul.

97

Investment Advice

The Context: 2 Peter 1:1–11

If you possess these qualities in increasing measure,
they will keep you from being ineffective and unproductive
in your knowledge of our Lord Jesus Christ. —Peter, 2 Peter 1:8

"I want to help you invest wisely in your future." That's what the financial advisor said as he began his talk about investing in 401(k)s and retirement funds. He wanted his listeners to continue putting money in the stock market during all the ups and downs of the economy because historically a good return will eventually occur.

God wants us to invest wisely in our spiritual future as well. Through the ups and downs of life's circumstances, we should continually invest in a "spiritual account": our character. The apostle Peter tells us to be diligent about character development (2 Peter 1:5–11). After we trust in Christ for salvation, we are to invest these qualities into our character: faith, virtue, knowledge, self-control, perseverance, godliness, brotherly kindness, and love.

The future returns on our investment in character will be godliness (vv. 5–7), fruitfulness in the knowledge of Jesus Christ (v. 8), assurance of our calling (v. 10), and victory over sin (v. 9).

Investing money in retirement funds can be profitable, but investing in our spiritual lives offers the best kind of return for our future!

Jesus Moment

What do you think being fruitful "in the knowledge of Jesus Christ" means? Could this knowledge unlock the secret to holy living for the believer? How can you increase in the knowledge of Christ?

_____

_____

_____

_____

_____

Action Steps

Give some thought to investing in your spiritual life.

- Investing in people. Are there men or women, boys or girls, teens or young adults who could use some of your time and interest? Even if you just encourage them with a kind word or a quick message, that action might reap benefits.

_____

_____

- Investing in church. How involved are you in the mission of your church? Being careful not to overextend yourself, is there anything you can do to assist what is happening there?

_____

_____

- Investing in yourself. Are you taking the time to pray and examine God's Word? Listen to Christian music for encouragement?

_____

_____

> Now is the time to invest in eternity.

98

I L-O-V-E . . .

The Context: Romans 6:1–11

Now if we died with Christ, we believe that we will also live with him.

—Paul, Romans 6:8

My husband and I were at a public swimming pool when the people around us started staring into the sky. A small plane was emitting smoke in the form of letters. As we watched, the pilot spelled out the letters: "I L-O-V-E." People began speculating: Maybe it was to be a marriage proposal. Perhaps a romantic man is standing nearby on a balcony with his girlfriend and will soon pop the Will-you-marry-me? question. We kept gazing upward: "I L-O-V-E Y-O-U J-E-." I heard young girls guessing: "I bet it will be Jen or maybe Jessica." He kept spelling. No. It was: "J-E-S-U-S." The pilot was declaring love for Jesus for many people to see.

A friend of mine often ends his prayers with "I love you, Lord." He says, "I can't help but say 'I love you' after all He's done for me." In Romans 6:1–11, our Bible reading for today, the apostle Paul tells us some of what Jesus has done for us that deserves our love: He was crucified, buried, and raised to life. Because of that, those of us who have put our faith in Jesus now have a new life (v. 4), we no longer have to be controlled by sin or fear of death (vv. 6, 9), and one day we too will be resurrected to live with Him forever (v. 8).

No wonder we say, "I love you, Jesus!"

Jesus Moment

We can't all be skywriters. What are some other ways you can say, "I love you, Jesus" so others will notice? Perhaps in how you treat others. In how you interact on social media. And in how you make time to worship Him. What are other ways?

_____

_____

_____

_____

Communicating with Jesus

In this prayer, fill in the blanks to insert specific reasons you say "I love you" to Jesus.

Dear Savior, I love you because you _____.
When I am afraid, you _____. When I don't
know which way to turn in life, you _____.
When I feel that my friends are too busy for me, I know that you
_____. Thank you for being my loving
Savior at all times and in all ways. I love you, and I owe my life
to you.

> To show His love, Jesus died for us;
> to show our love, we live for Him.

99

Take the Time

The Context: Luke 19:1–10

Come down immediately. I must stay at your house today.
—Jesus, Luke 19:5

Rima, a Syrian woman who had recently moved to the United States, tried to explain to her tutor with hand motions and limited English why she was upset. Tears trickled down her cheeks as she held up a beautifully arranged platter of *fatayer* (meat, cheese, and spinach pies) that she had made. Then she said, "One man," and made a swishing sound as she pointed from the door to the living room and then back to the door. The tutor pieced together that several people from a nearby church were supposed to visit Rima and her family and bring some gifts. But only one man had shown up. He had hurried in, dropped off a box of items, and rushed out. He was busy taking care of a responsibility, while she and her family were lonely and longed for community and to share their *fatayer* with new friends.

Taking time for people is what Jesus was all about. He attended dinner parties, taught crowds, and took time for interaction with individuals. He even invited himself to one man's house. Zacchaeus, a tax collector, climbed a tree to see Him, and when Jesus looked up, He said, "Come down immediately. I must stay at your house today" (Luke 19:1–9). And Zacchaeus's life was changed forever.

Because of other responsibilities, we won't always be able to take the time. But when we do, we have a wonderful privilege of being with others and watching the Lord work through us.

Jesus Moment

Jesus was multitasking a little. He was passing through town (Luke 19:1), yet He was also looking for a person who needed Him. How can you find "Jesus-needing people" as you pass through life?

_____

_____

_____

_____

_____

Thinking about Hospitality

Answer these true-or-false questions about making time with others and hospitality based on real life, not some idealized view of things:

_____ In order to practice hospitality, I have to have a big, fancy house that looks like it was built for a movie star.

_____ People really don't care what you have; they want to know that you care.

_____ The most important thing to do after church on Sunday is to rush out of the building to have lunch.

_____ It is not my responsibility to start up conversations with others; people need to approach me first.

The best gift you can give to others may be your time.

100

The Kindness Man

The Context: Luke 7:11–17

When the Lord saw her, his heart went out to her.
—Luke, Luke 7:13

Disillusioned and wanting a more meaningful life, Leon quit his job in finance. Then one day he saw a homeless man holding up this sign at a street corner: KINDNESS IS THE BEST MEDICINE. Leon says, "Those words rammed straight into me. It was an epiphany."

Leon decided to begin his new life by creating an international organization to promote kindness. He travels around the world, relying on strangers to provide him with food, gas, and a place to stay. Then he rewards them, through his organization, with good deeds such as feeding orphans or building on to a school for underprivileged children. He says, "It's sometimes seen as being soft. But kindness is a profound strength."

Christ's very essence as God is goodness, so kindness naturally flowed from Him. I love the story of what Jesus did when He came upon the funeral procession of a widow's only son (Luke 7:11–17). The grieving woman most likely was dependent on her son for financial support. We don't read in the story that anyone asked Jesus to intervene. Purely from the goodness of His nature (v. 13), He was concerned and brought her son back to life. The people said of Christ, "God has come to help his people" (v. 16).

Jesus Moment

How can you be Jesus to someone when no one else around seems to care for those who need help? Which organizations in your church or community need a "Kindness Woman" to do on a smaller scale what Leon did internationally in Jesus's name?

_____

_____

_____

_____

_____

Inspiring Words

"As long as you can sweeten another's pain, life is not in vain."
—Helen Keller, American author (1880–1968)

"Any definition of a successful life must include serving others."
—George H. W. Bush, American president (1924–2018)

"No one has ever become poor by giving."
—Anne Frank, German writer (1929–1945)

> Without Christ there is no hope.

Help us get the word out!

Our Daily Bread Publishing exists to feed the soul with the Word of God.

If you appreciated this book, please let others know.

- Pick up another copy to give as a gift.

- Share a link to the book or mention it on social media.

- Write a review on your blog, on a book-seller's website, or at our own site (odb.org/store).

- Recommend this book for your church, book club, or small group.

Connect with us:

 @ourdailybread

 @ourdailybread

@ourdailybread

Our Daily Bread Publishing
PO Box 3566
Grand Rapids, Michigan 49501 USA

 books@odb.org